What people

Disordered Minds

This brilliant book, pulls together a big picture like no other books on psychopaths and politics I've seen. Further, it addresses, like no other book I've found, the damage that is caused when what Hughes calls "the toxic Triangle" enables psychopaths to gain power at a national level. This is a book that legislators and leaders should read.

Rob Kall, Founder of OpEdNews, host of the Bottom Up Radio Show and author of *Bottom Up: The Connection Revolution*

Ian Hughes' fascinating book makes us reflect on the importance of electing leaders who are not just inspiring and effective but have a balanced personality. He has convinced me that every potential leader will one day have to publish not only their manifesto but also their psychological profile.

Graham Farmelo, Costa Book Award Winner, LA Times Book Prizes Winner and author of *Churchill's Bomb: A Hidden Story of Science, Politics and War,* and *The Strangest Man: The Hidden Life of Paul Dirac, Quantum Genius*

As one of the most impressive and respected multidisciplinary scientists today, Ian Hughes in *Disordered Minds* gives a compelling and timely account of the dangers posed by psychologically dangerous leaders and provides a stark warning that the conditions in which this psychopathy flourishes – extremes of social inequality and a culture of hyper-individualism – are very much the hallmarks of our present age. A must read!

Professor Frederick M. Burkle, Jr, MD, Senior Fellow & Scientist, Harvard University, author of *Antisocial Personality Disorder and Pathological Narcissism in Prolonged Conflicts and Wars of the 21st Century, DMPHP, 2015*

An excellent account of how malignant narcissism is evident in the lives of the great dictators, and how the conditions in which this psychopathy flourishes have returned to haunt us. *Disordered Minds* serves as a clear warning that tyrants such as Hitler, Stalin and Mao should not be seen simply as historical figures, but rather as dangerous contemporaries, as modern people, closer to us than we might like to think, who can tell us something vital about our dangerous present and our uncertain future.

Dr Kieran Keohane, Senior Lecturer in Sociology, University College Cork and editor of *The Social Pathologies of Contemporary Civilization*

Ian Hughes explains with admirable clarity and ease the ways in which dangerous individuals can emerge, flourish and dominate others in certain social and political settings, causing untold harm, violence and barbarism. In an age of right-wing 'illiberal democracy', xenophobic populism and the rise of politicians such as Trump in the U.S. or Le Pen in France, *Disordered Minds* is a diagnostic tool with which to identify both the social disorders and personality disorders that can threaten hard won democratic freedoms and undermine moves towards building a less unequal society and securing basic socio-economic rights for all. As we search for answers to explain our troubled times, we should be grateful to Ian Hughes for writing this book.

John Barry, Professor of Green Political Economy, Queen's University Belfast and author of *The Politics of Actually Existing Unsustainability: Human Flourishing in a Climate-Changed, Carbon Constrained World*

Ian Hughes adds new scientific insight to one of the deepest conundrums of politics: that positions of power appeal to the narcissistic, paranoid psychopaths among us, with catastrophic results for humanity. His argument that human institutions, particularly liberal democracy, are needed to constrain the

worst of human nature, is profound and (needless to say) timely. *Disordered Minds* is sometimes disturbing, but it is consistently fascinating, and ultimately constructive and hopeful.
Steven Pinker, Johnstone Professor of Psychology, Harvard University, and the author of *The Better Angels of Our Nature* and *Enlightenment Now*

Ian Hughes' book *Disordered Minds* is essential reading in the era of Donald Trump. Hughes explains with insight and eloquence how leaders with disordered minds – psychopathy, narcissism, and paranoia – can take control in unstable societies and create mass movements that empower other disordered minds as well. The results can be disastrous: murder, mayhem, starvation, and war. Hughes emphasizes not only the threats of today's mega-greed and massive inequality but solutions as well, including democratic institutions, a social democratic ethos, and the global movement towards sustainable development.
Professor Jeffrey Sachs, Columbia University

However they are formed, our world produces them – the psychopaths and those with narcissistic or paranoid personality disorders. You have met them, worked with them, maybe even lived with them or been victimized by them and you know just how bafflingly plausible they can be and how disastrously evil. *Disordered Minds* introduces us to the vast wastelands they are capable of creating when you and I, our neighbors, friends, families and colleagues fail to see just how dangerous they are, when we fail to underpin our democracies with the infrastructures capable of withstanding the onslaught of the deceptively charismatic lunatic leader. Read this exceptionally fine and accessible work of scholarship and make it your business to keep their disordered minds from disordering our universe.
Mary McAleese, Former President of Ireland

Disordered Minds

How Dangerous Personalities Are
Destroying Democracy

Disordered Minds

How Dangerous Personalities Are Destroying Democracy

Ian Hughes

Winchester, UK
Washington, USA

First published by Zero Books, 2018
Zero Books is an imprint of John Hunt Publishing Ltd., No. 3 East St., Alresford,
Hampshire SO24 9EE, UK
office1@jhpbooks.net
www.johnhuntpublishing.com
www.zero-books.net

For distributor details and how to order please visit the 'Ordering' section on our website.

Text copyright: Ian Hughes 2017

ISBN: 978 1 78535 880 7
978 1 78535 881 4 (ebook)
Library of Congress Control Number: 2017957123

A CIP catalogue record for this book is available from the British Library.

Design: Stuart Davies

Printed and bound by CPI Group (UK) Ltd, Croydon, CR0 4YY, UK

We operate a distinctive and ethical publishing philosophy in
all areas of our business, from our global network of authors to
production and worldwide distribution.

Contents

For
Kay and Sam
Love never ends

Acknowledgments

Isaac Newton famously said that if he had seen further it was by standing on the shoulders of giants. I would like to begin by acknowledging the many authors upon whose work I have drawn and who are cited in this book's references.

Many friends and colleagues have contributed to this work by reading drafts and discussing the book's arguments as the manuscript evolved. I owe an enormous debt to Tom Arnold, Helmut Beck, Doug Bennett, Frederick Burkle, James Colgan, Sandy Dunlop, Geraint Ellis, Graham Farmelo, Sean Gough, Kitty Holland, Therese Hume, Jason Jiang, Rob Kall, William Kerr, Steen Kristensen, Paula Maguire, Cathy Moore, Barry O'Connell, Elizabeth Mika, Ellen O'Malley Dunlop, Henry McDonald, Kate O'Neill, Raymond O'Neill, Joachim Pietsch, John Sutton, Alan Taylor, Brian Trench, and Rachael Weiss. Particular thanks are due to friends Grainne Murphy, Alan Villaver, Pat Nolan, Sean O'Driscoll, and Roger Duck.

John Barry, Jan Rosier, Kieran Keohane, and Sylda Langford played pivotal roles at various points in the process. My sincere gratitude to all of you.

I am extremely lucky to have as my agent Tracy Brennan whose inspiration and support go beyond the call of duty. Tracy has been a true partner in making this book happen.

Special thanks to the staff at Zero Books, especially Doug Lain, John Romans, and Trevor Greenfield. I owe a special debt of gratitude to John Hunt for his belief in this book from day one.

Finally, special thanks to my mother, the earth on which I walk, and to my siblings and extended family. Their love and encouragement are the bedrock of my life and career. This book would not have been written without them.

In my last conversation with my father before he passed away, he asked me how this book was progressing. 'I'm working on it', I said. 'You'd better get on with it', was his reply. Here it is Dad. This is for you.

Introduction

In my earliest memory I am holding my father's hand. He towers above me as we walk across the gravel in the fading evening light toward the television room at the caravan park where we are holidaying on the southwest coast of Ireland. It is the summer of 1969. We are going to watch together the first human ever to set foot on the surface of another world. A few small steps for man and boy, a giant leap for mankind. Fast forward 10 years and my father gave me a book on astronomy that he himself had read as a child. I still remember distinctly the impact that reading the sentence, 'Every star is a sun' had on me. It was as if the sky had cracked wide open. That night, when the stars came out, I was aware for the first time of the immensity and wonder of the universe into which I had been born.

Tragically, the summer of 1969 also witnessed a giant leap backwards, as my hometown, and all of Northern Ireland, descended into the barbarity of 'the Troubles'. Over the next 3 decades more than 3,600 people were killed as bombings and shootings became an almost daily occurrence. This book has grown out of my experience of growing up in such a violent society. It is rooted in a childish passion to make sense of how violence can coexist with wonder.

Outline of the Book

A personality disorder is a type of mental disorder characterized by a rigid and unhealthy pattern of thinking, functioning, and behaving. Most personality disorders, such a depressive disorder and obsessive-compulsive disorder, cause distress to the person suffering from the condition, rather than posing a danger to others. Of all the personality disorders recognized by psychiatrists, this book is concerned with only three – psychopathy, narcissistic personality disorder, and paranoid

3

personality disorder. People who suffer from these disorders pose a very real danger to society.

Chapter 1: 'Disordered Minds' describes what we know about dangerous personality disorders. The chapter develops the book's first argument: that people with these disorders pose a grave threat to society when they act together and when the circumstances are such that they can influence a substantial proportion of the psychologically normal population to support them.

Chapter 2: 'Stalin and Mao' and Chapter 3: 'Hitler and Pol Pot' provide concrete examples of this dynamic in practice. These chapters use a model called the 'toxic triangle', comprising destructive leaders, susceptible followers, and conducive environments, to illustrate how people with these disorders come to power. These chapters show that the history of the twentieth century cannot be understood without acknowledging the central role that people with these disorders played in fomenting the century's most tragic events.

Chapter 4: 'Democracy as Defense' introduces the book's second main argument, namely that democracy can be understood as a system of defenses against people with these disorders. This system of defenses comprises the rule of law, electoral democracy, the principle of liberal individualism, social democracy, and legal protection for human rights. Acting together, this system of defenses serves as a deterrent against dangerous individuals, while democracy also creates ethical norms under which the majority of us are less likely to support them.

Chapter 5: 'Destroying Democracy' argues that democracy remains fragile today because the conditions which empower this dangerous minority are still deeply embedded in our political, economic, and religious institutions. These conditions include vast inequalities in wealth and the culture of excessive greed which have come to characterize modern capitalism.

Despite the violence and greed that currently scar our world, there are grounds for optimism. These are set out in Chapter 6: 'Hope?' Democracy has been spreading and deepening over time. As a result, many parts of the world today enjoy a greater level of protection against psychopathic, narcissistic, and paranoid leaders than in any previous era. Reasons for hope can also be found in our psychology. Dangerous personality disorders are, at least in part, the result of failures in love and care in early childhood. Finding ways to reduce the occurrence of such disorders, while strengthening societies' defenses against those who suffer from them, can lead us to a more just and peaceful world.

Much more, however, remains to be done. The existential threats that humanity faces at this moment in history are very real. So the book closes by introducing a fourth argument. At the beginning of the twenty-first century a strengthening of democracy is urgently required if human progress is to continue, immense human suffering is to be avoided, and perhaps even if humanity is to survive, in the decades to come.

Why This Book Matters

There are three reasons why this book matters. First, the concept of personality disorder is generally not well understood. This book aims to clarify what these disorders are and to show, given the difficulties in conclusively identifying individuals with these disorders, that a more nuanced and effective approach to public diagnosis is needed.

Second, by explaining how democracy can be understood as a system of defenses against dangerous personalities, this book provides a new and vital psychological perspective on democracy. At a time when democracy itself is in retreat worldwide, it explains clearly what democracy is and why it is crucially important that we defend it.

Third, this book matters because the malign influence of a

minority of people with dangerous personality disorders is causing the rest of us to believe in a distorted view of our own nature. We are not an irredeemably violent and greedy species. The majority of people the world over crave peace, justice, and freedom from oppression and discrimination. It is only by reducing the influence of the minority with these disorders that we will begin to see this truth more clearly.

My experience of growing up in a violent society taught me a fundamental fact that most textbooks do not – when it comes to our propensity for violence and greed, human beings are not all the same. This assertion is at odds with the predominant paradigm in psychology today which assumes that, because every person is capable of violence and greed, we are all equal in this respect. Growing up it was clear to me that people like my father were of a different moral order to those who relished their roles as bullies and thugs, empowered by nationalism and religion to commit atrocity after atrocity. The discovery of dangerous personality disorders finally provides us with scientific evidence that when it comes to violence and greed we are not all the same.

1. Disordered Minds

Civilization's Thin Veneer

The practice of violence changes the world, but the most probable change is a more violent world.

Hannah Arendt

For anyone interested in psychology, a visit to the Freud Museum in Vienna is a chance to walk in the footsteps of one of the greatest explorers of the human mind. For students of history it is a reminder of some of Europe's darkest days. Sigmund Freud, a non-practising Jew, was allowed to leave Vienna in 1938 by the Nazi authorities after intense lobbying by friends in England. Four of Freud's sisters were not so fortunate. They died in the concentration camps of Auschwitz, Treblinka, and Theresienstadt. Mercifully Freud never learned their fate. He died at the age of 83, just days before Hitler's invasion of Poland and the outbreak of World War Two in Europe.

W.H. Auden, in his poem *In Memory of Sigmund Freud*, commended Freud for inventing psychoanalysis as a means of exploring the hidden regions of the human psyche. In the poem Auden compares Freud implicitly with Jesus for relieving the suffering of the afflicted by walking among the destitute and the lowly.

Freud would have been amused by Auden's implicit comparison. In *Civilisation and Its Discontents*, Freud took issue with Jesus for the naivety of his commandment, 'Love thy neighbour as thyself.' In light of the events unfolding around the world in 1938, particularly the brutal anti-Semitism he was observing daily in Vienna, Freud saw such a commandment as flying directly in the face of human reality. 'Not merely is this stranger in general unworthy of my love;' Freud wrote, 'I must honestly confess that he has more claim to my hostility and even my hatred...[I]f he can satisfy any sort of desire by it, he thinks nothing of jeering at me, insulting me, slandering me, and showing his superior power; and the more secure he feels and the more helpless I am, the more certainly I can expect him to behave like this to me.'[1]

Later in the same essay Freud concludes, 'The time comes when each one of us has to give up as illusions the expectations which, in his youth, he pinned upon his fellow-men, and when he may learn how much difficulty and pain has been added to his life by their ill-will.'[2]

Decades after Freud's death, the philosopher Hannah Arendt, like Freud a Jewish refugee from Nazi Germany, covered the trial of Adolf Eichmann for the *New Yorker* magazine. Her articles created a storm of protest. Eichmann, a former SS Corporal in Dachau, was the man responsible for designing the system of transport that was used to carry millions to their deaths in the concentration camps. In describing Eichmann, she used the phrase 'banality of evil'. It is important to understand what she meant. 'When I speak of the banality of evil, I do so only on the strictly factual level, pointing to a phenomenon which stared one in the face at the trial...' she wrote. 'Except for an extraordinary diligence in looking out for his personal advancement, he had no motives at all. He merely, to put the matter colloquially, never realized what he was doing...'[3] For Eichmann it seems, sending millions of men, women, and children to their agonising deaths in the gas chambers had the same emotional impact as casting wood on a fire.

Arendt's coverage of Eichmann's trial suggests that the most horrendous acts of evil can be perpetrated by the most normal-seeming people. Her phrase 'the banality of evil' implies that we all have the potential to become monsters. This is a view with which Freud would have agreed. In *Civilisation and Its Discontents* he wrote, '...the inclination to aggression is an original, self-subsisting instinctual disposition in man...'[4] It is also a common view among contemporary psychologists. Philip Zimbardo, Professor of Psychology at Stanford University, for example, has written, 'Those people who become perpetrators of evil deeds and those who become perpetrators of heroic deeds are basically alike, in being just ordinary, average people.'[5]

Modern psychology, however, challenges the idea that we are all equally capable of violence and greed. While history clearly shows that ordinary people can, and do, participate in acts of atrocity, modern psychiatry is revealing that a small but significant minority have an innate and seemingly unalterable ability to treat others with brutality and disdain, of a different order to that of the majority. The presence of this minority distorts our societies and shifts the predominant values of humanity away from non-violence, compromise, and compassion, toward brutality, confrontation, and greed. In much the same way that adding a small amount of carbon to iron produces a much harder material, steel, so the presence of the small proportion of people who suffer from dangerous personality disorders fundamentally alters the timbre of humanity, at immense cost to us all.

How Early Relationships Shape Whom We Become

Since Freud's time, three core ideas have become central to psychoanalytic thought.

The first is that, as infants, we develop best in an environment of love and fun.

The second is that our internal worlds are formed in early childhood and have an enduring influence on our relationships throughout our lives.

And the third idea is that much of the suffering in the world can be traced to neglect and abuse in childhood.

Psychoanalysts since Freud have passionately believed that

these ideas have the power to change our lives and reshape our world. Now neuroscience and biochemistry are showing that, on these key ideas at least, Freud was right.

Over the last few decades, neuroscientists have shown conclusively that the development of a baby's brain depends critically on the quality of the physical and emotional care it receives.[6] As psychotherapist and author Sue Gerhardt explains, babies come into the world with a need for social interaction to develop and organize their brains. If they do not get enough empathic, attuned attention, then important parts of their brains simply do not develop as well as they should.[7]

And the consequences of poor brain development in infancy can be severe. They can include a reduced capacity for empathy and love, difficulties in interpersonal relationships, and, in some cases, the development of dangerous personality disorders that are marked by a higher propensity for violence and greed.

So how do early relationships shape our brains? One region that plays a key role in emotional life is the orbitofrontal cortex, which is situated at the front of the brain just above our eye sockets. Our capacity to empathize and to engage in emotional communication with other people requires a developed orbitofrontal cortex. People with damage in this region cannot relate sensitively toward others. Scientists now know that the orbitofrontal cortex develops almost entirely after birth. What is more, it does not develop solely according to a predetermined genetic blueprint. Instead the way in which it develops, and the neural connections which are made within it, and between it and other parts of the brain, depend critically on caring relationships in our early years.

Pleasurable interactions – whether a loving gaze, shared laughter, or a warm embrace – arouse the infant's nervous system and heart rate, triggering the release of vital biochemicals. In this way, love and fun produce the chemicals that help the baby's brain to grow. The absence of such emotional stimulation deprives the child of the chemicals needed for normal brain growth. In babies who have been subject to early emotional or physical abuse, the orbitofrontal cortex has been found to be significantly smaller in volume.

The volume of the frontal part of the brain, however, is not the only thing that matters. How well the neurons are connected up within the pre-frontal cortex is also crucial, particularly the connections that are formed between the left and right sides of the baby's brain. Between 6 and 12 months after birth, a massive burst of synaptic connections occurs within the brain, connecting up the right and left hemispheres. The two hemispheres have different modes of operation. The left carries out specialized functions related to logic and verbal processing; the right is specialized in functions related to emotion. The interconnections formed between the two parts of the brain in infancy mean that our adult mind is able to draw on the resources of the left brain to regulate feelings. Similarly, the logical cognitive processes of the left brain can be informed by emotional reality. In the absence of love and play in our early years, however, the left and right brain will not be as well connected, resulting, once again, in adverse consequences for our emotional and mental health.

The second core idea of psychoanalysis is that our internal worlds are formed in early childhood and have an enduring influence on our relationships throughout our lives.

'Object relations' is one influential school of psychoanalysis. Psychoanalysts of this school have long argued that our internal worlds are fragmented and are comprised of multiple 'internal objects' that determine how we relate to ourselves and others. The term 'internal object' essentially means a mental and emotional image of another person, or part of another person (such as a smiling face), that has been taken inside the self. Our most important internal objects are those derived from our parents in early childhood.

According to object relations theory, when we interact with

other people, these internal objects are activated. Depending on whether our internal world is dominated by images of fear and danger, or images of love and care, our internal objects strongly influence how we relate to others. Over the last few decades, neuroscientists have been discovering evidence that supports object relations theory. We have seen how the early development of an infant's brain involves an explosion of synaptic connections which link together different parts of the baby's brain. Initially these connections are made in a chaotic fashion. Then, as a result of the infant's experiences, particular connections begin to solidify. Out of the chaotic overproduction of connections, patterns start to emerge. The baby's most frequent and repetitive experiences result in well-trodden neural pathways, while those neural connections which lie unused begin to fade away. In this way, the baby's most typical experiences shape the networks of connections within its brain.

As the brain develops further, images and words accumulate within these neural networks. Between 12 and 18 months of age, when the baby begins to develop a capacity for storing images, an inner library of pictures also begins to be built up. Both positive and negative images and interactions are remembered and stored. During the baby's second year, as the child's verbal ability develops rapidly, words start to play as big a role as physical and visual communication. Words too, saturated with emotion, are stored as part of the child's neural networks. When these networks are activated through interactions with others, the dense webs of interconnections invoke rich associations of images, words, and emotions, and provide the infant with a practical guide to action. As psychoanalysts have long held, these neural networks – or 'internal objects' – underpin our behavior and our expectations of others throughout our lives, often without our realizing it.

Neuroscience, then, has shown conclusively that the absence of loving relationships in infancy can result in a smaller brain volume and a scarcity of neural connections within the brain. It has also shown that the patterns of behavior we experience in early childhood become hard wired into our brains and influence how we relate to others throughout our lives. The consequences of poor brain development resulting from adverse childhood experiences can last a lifetime and can include lack of empathy, rigidity in beliefs and behaviors, difficulties in relating to others, and the development of a host of disorders of personality.

Which brings us to psychoanalysis' third core idea, namely that much of the suffering in this world can be traced to neglect and abuse in childhood.

Three disorders of personality are now known to predispose an individual to violent or excessively selfish behavior. These disorders are psychopathy, narcissistic personality disorder, and paranoid personality disorder. While the precise cause of these disorders is still disputed, it is highly likely that physically or emotionally abusive relationships in infancy and childhood contribute to their development.

Of course, not every child who experiences neglect and abuse will develop a dangerous personality disorder. The resilience of the human spirit sees to that. But a minority do. And as we shall see, that minority plays a critical role in the violence and greed that deforms our world.

Dangerous Personality Disorders

For decades a steady stream of psychologists has been raising the alarm on the devastating effect that people with certain personality disorders are having on society. *The Mask of Sanity*[8] first published in 1941 by Hervey Cleckley, Robert Linder's study *Rebel Without a Cause*[9] from 1944, Theodore Millon's 1981 *Disorders of Personality*[10], and Robert Hare's more recent *Without Conscience*[11] have been sounding a series of clear and persistent warnings. All of these authors warn that the destruction wreaked by psychopaths and those with certain other dangerous personality disorders is vastly underestimated.

So what are dangerous personality disorders? Up to 12 personality disorders have been recognized by the international psychiatric community. It is important to emphasize that not all of these personality disorders are dangerous and correlate with an increased risk of harmful behavior toward others. Indeed, most personality disorders result solely in distress and social hardship for the person suffering from the disorder. Such is the case, for example, with obsessive-compulsive personality disorder and depressive personality disorder.

Of all the recognized personality disorders, this book is concerned with only three. People with these three types of dangerous personality disorder – psychopathy, narcissistic personality disorder, and paranoid personality disorder – are proven to be much more likely to be involved in violence and criminality. Dangerous personality disorders are deeply engrained and enduring patterns of behavior that represent extreme deviations from the way the average person thinks, feels, and relates to others. They manifest as rigid patterns of behavior that are difficult, threatening, and harmful to others, including an increased propensity for violence and greed. In fact, people with these disorders are up to ten times more likely to have a criminal conviction than those without.[12] People with these disorders suffer from distortions in the basic cognitive and emotional structures of their minds. These distortions include deficits in basic emotional functioning, such as the absence of feelings toward others, and cognitive distortions, such as the inability to process any information that runs counter to their inflated self-image. While everyone can manifest callous, narcissistic, and paranoid traits, depending on circumstances, it is the rigidity of their thoughts and feelings that marks people with dangerous disorders out from the majority of the population.

Psychopaths

a babe, by intercourse of touch
I held mute dialogs with my mother's heart
Wordsworth

A human being is something that evokes feelings in another human being. This fact can serve as our most basic definition of what a human being is. As we have seen, research in psychology and neuroscience is showing how the mute emotional dialogs with our mothers' and fathers' hearts, which Wordsworth describes in his epic poem *Prelude*, are the very process that molds the tone and structure of our minds. From our earliest days, to perceive others' feelings is to react with feelings of our own. Infants only a few weeks old react to joy in their mother's face with increased joy of their own; they react to sadness in their mother's face by becoming sad and subdued themselves; they react to anger with anger of their own. These emotional dialogs mean that, as infants, we quickly learn that the difference between people and things is that things do not engage with us in emotional communication.

However, for some people the vital distinction between the world of people and the world of things fails to develop. Such people, those with psychopathic personalities, are not capable of reacting to other people's feelings with feelings of their own. As a result, psychopaths have a terrifying ability to treat people without conscience. And what happens when human beings act toward others as if they were not people but things? The disturbing answer lies in the mindlessly violent behavior of psychopaths.

Leading expert Martha Stout gives the following description of the psychopath:

'Imagine – if you can – not having a conscience, none at all, no feelings of guilt or remorse no matter what you do, no limiting sense of concern for the well-being of strangers, friends or even family members. Imagine no struggles with shame, not a single one in your whole life, no matter what kind of selfish, lazy, harmful or immoral action you had taken...You are not held back from any of your desires by guilt or shame, and you are never confronted by others for your cold-bloodedness. The ice water in your veins is so bizarre, so completely outside of their personal experience that they seldom even guess at your condition...How will you live your life? What will you do with your huge and secret advantage, and with the corresponding handicap of other people (conscience)?'[13]

The behavior of people with psychopathic personality disorder is often incomprehensible to those with a normal psychological make-up. Psychologist Robert Hare, one of the leading authorities on this disorder, gives the following examples of psychopathic behavior: the woman who encouraged her boyfriend to rape her 5-year-old daughter anytime she herself did not feel like having sex; the mother who accidently injured herself while shooting dead her three young children, and who later complained that her greatest regret was that her injury meant that she couldn't bend to tie her shoelaces; the man who, realising that he had left his wallet at home, robbed the nearest petrol station by smashing the attendant unconscious with a plank of wood rather than suffer the inconvenience of returning home; and the convicted murderer who killed on his first day of release from prison just to see what it felt like to kill someone again.

It is not only the behavior of psychopaths that is beyond the comprehension of psychologically normal people – their thinking is too. As we have seen, emotional development – the mute dialogs with our mother's and father's hearts – provides the essential bedrock for the neural wiring in our brains and the development of cognitive abilities. Without this basic emotional foundation in place, the development of our ability to think is likely to be severely impaired. It is not surprising then that so fundamental an emotional deficit as the complete lack of ability to register and respond to other people's emotions brings with it severe disabilities in cognition. Psychopaths frequently suffer from a chilling inability to recognize the suffering they have caused others. This can be seen, for example, in the case of a serial rapist who believed that his victims would be grateful to him for helping get their names in the newspapers, or the serial murderer who killed over 30 young men and described how, looking back, he saw himself 'more as a victim than a perpetrator.'[14]

Psychopaths pose a grave danger to society because of their propensity for extreme behaviors, including violent crime and fraud. According to Hare, half of all serious crime is committed by psychopaths.[15] There is some evidence to suggest that violent crimes committed by psychopaths differ in nature from those committed by non-psychopathic offenders. While violent crimes by non-psychopathic people are usually fueled by emotion – jealousy, hatred or greed – and are likely to be targeted at people known to the perpetrator, the violence of psychopaths is more often dispassionate, unprovoked violence committed against victims of convenience. Two-thirds of the victims of psychopathic killers are random strangers.[16]

There is much we do not understand about psychopathy, and debate is still raging within the psychiatric profession regarding how psychopathy should be defined. The most recent research suggests that there may even be two distinct types of psychopath.

The main clinical instrument currently used for diagnosis, a questionnaire known as the Psychopathy Checklist, Revised (PCL-R), was designed for use with criminal populations and includes items such as juvenile delinquency and criminal history as part of the diagnosis. Almost everything we currently know about psychopathy comes from research using the PCL-R on prison populations. As a result, the strong impression is that psychopathic individuals inevitably commit violent crimes. This may not be so.

Early conceptions of psychopathy, including that of the pioneer in this area, Harvey Cleckley, did not characterize psychopaths as being explosively violent, predatory, or cruel. Instead, Cleckley believed that the harm that psychopaths caused came about as a secondary consequence of their inability to feel empathy toward others. This means that individuals with this condition may not automatically become killers or fraudsters.[17] Indeed it appears that some psychopaths can choose whether or not to engage in criminal activity. These so called 'successful psychopaths' are more likely, it appears, to manifest their callousness through involvement in professions such as business, law, and politics, than to engage in violence.

The view that psychopathy does not inevitably lead to violence finds tentative support in recent research which shows that, using the PCL-R, those diagnosed as psychopathic fall into two different groups. The individuals in one group generally comply with the classic conception of psychopaths as cold and emotionless, while those in the second group are much more anxious, hot-headed and emotionally volatile. Although seemingly different in character, these two subgroups both obtain high scores in the PCL-R. This finding suggests that individuals in the anxious, emotionally volatile group may be a greater risk for committing violence than those with classic cold-blooded psychopathy.

Narcissists

A second type of personality disorder that is associated with a higher risk of anti-social behavior is narcissistic personality disorder.

The characteristics of narcissistic personality disorder are well known: a grandiose sense of self-importance or uniqueness; an exhibitionistic need for constant attention and admiration; a lack of empathy and an inability to recognize how others feel; disregard for the personal integrity and rights of others; and relationships marked by a sense of entitlement and the exploitation of others.

It can be argued that until relatively recently narcissism formed the very basis of human relations. Throughout history it was widely accepted that people were inherently unequal. Kings ruled by divine right and the nobility were deemed to be superior to the masses. For millennia, to question those at the top of the social hierarchy was seen as a rebellion against nature and the will of God. It was only at the beginning of the modern era that the idea of equality began to replace the rigidities of class, gender, and hereditary privilege. Research into personality disorders, however, shows clearly that not everyone is psychologically capable of conceptualizing the idea of equality. There are people – those with narcissistic personality disorder – whose minds are structured to convince them of their own superiority and for whom the idea of equality is literally inconceivable.

Contrary to popular belief, it is not narcissistic for a person to value a quality in himself which he actually possesses, or to want to be admired and valued by others. The problem is that narcissists love and admire themselves for qualities for which there is no adequate foundation. Their apparent self-confidence arises from the fact that their mental stability depends on their believing in, and projecting, an image of superiority. The myth of Narcissus powerfully conveys this core feature of narcissistic personality disorder. The myth tells us how the handsome Narcissus was doted on by the nymph Echo, only to have him reject her advances. In retaliation, the gods decided to punish Narcissus by making him fall in love with his own reflection in a mountain pool. Every time Narcissus reached out to his own perfect image, however, the image fragmented, causing him to die of sadness. As the myth conveys, the core of narcissistic personality disorder is the obsession with an image of perfection and the absence of an authentic sense of self-worth. The narcissist's deep insecurity compels him to engage in continual exhibitionism, seeking constant attention and approval. But like the child who fears his exhibitionism will be met with ridicule, the narcissist is constantly living in fear of humiliation and shame. Should his perfect image of himself be exposed as a sham, he, like Narcissus, would die of sadness. More often, however, he flies into fits of narcissistic rage in order to keep his unstable personality structure intact.

A quirk of their psychology also means that narcissists can come across as intelligent and articulate. Because of their absolute conviction that they are always right, narcissists seldom trouble themselves with understanding other people's views. They are often incapable of listening and synthesizing others' ideas with their own in order to create something new. Bereft of creativity, they excel as masters of destruction. In discussion and debate, their objective is not to reach a rational or objective conclusion, or to work together to reach a compromise. Their objective is simply to demonstrate their own superiority. Hence their danger to democratic politics and forms of decision-making based on deliberation, debate, and compromise and the willingness to change one's mind based on the force of a better argument. Unburdened by all of the normal constraints of listening and processing, they simply adopt the tactic of questioning their opponent's every statement and devising counter-arguments that expose the flaws in their opponent's views. Generally, narcissists do not hold onto any particular belief or consistent position, except one – the belief that they are superior to others. They can therefore constantly shift their stated position and adhere to this altered position as doggedly as before. This combination of rigid certainty (they are superior and therefore must be right) and blatant inconsistency (shifting their position moment to moment) makes it extremely difficult for others to counteract their arguments. As a result, narcissists often come across as being intelligent, articulate, and skilful negotiators – the ultimate triumph of style over substance.[18] The narcissist's belief that they are always right and others are always wrong means that they invariably dismiss other people's views with contempt. Anyone who dares to disagree with them shows themselves to be not only intellectually inferior, but also as having the impertinence to question their superior knowledge. They are therefore likely to react to anyone who challenges them with active or passive aggression.

Narcissists are capable of empathy and under normal circumstances may be less likely to engage in the casual violence that typifies some psychopaths. Even in the absence of violence on their part, however, by rigidly adhering to their own self-righteous superiority and refusing to yield to reasonable demands for the sharing of power and resources, narcissists often create the conditions in which violence becomes inevitable.

Narcissists exert a disproportionate influence on society because a number of characteristics of narcissistic personality disorder mean that they are more likely to reach positions of authority than those with normal psychology. Their abiding self-confidence, their absolute certainty in their beliefs and abilities, and their sense of entitlement to positions of authority over others, mean that they pursue power and authority with a passion that most others lack. Their energy, doggedness, and drive – which mask an overpowering need to triumph and an inability to accept defeat – often propel them to positions of power.

Current estimates are that narcissistic personality disorder affects around 1 percent of the general population. Given their particular skills, and the value placed on competitiveness and triumph in many societies, narcissists can be expected to make up a much higher proportion of those in positions of power.

Paranoia

Thoughts are the shadows of our sensations – always darker, emptier, simpler than these.
Neitzsche

A third personality disorder associated with a higher risk of violence is paranoid personality disorder. Just as narcissists are incapable of conceiving others as their equals, people with paranoid personality disorder are incapable of seeing others as anything but a threat.

We have seen how as infants we evoke emotion in others and respond to others' emotions with emotions of our own. Pioneering psychoanalyst Wilfred Bion developed a picture of how these basic emotions form the building blocks for thoughts.[19] According to Bion, our instinctive emotional reactions are the starting points for thoughts, but they need to be further developed by the mind in order to form connected thoughts and thinking. However, our minds can be either open to the process of registering our emotional feelings and processing them further into thoughts, or they can be closed to such a process. Whether or not we are in a state of mind to process emotional reactions into thoughts is the key determinant of our ability to think.

In her work with disturbed children, Melanie Klein, another leading psychoanalyst, discovered that as babies we exhibit two main states of mind, each with its own mood music and its own aptitude for thinking and learning. In the first state of mind – the paranoid state – the baby feels threatened and is terrified that she is about to be attacked. In order to avoid being overcome with fear, the baby shuts off her awareness of her emotions. In this paranoid state of mind, emotions cannot be held and processed into thoughts. Given the reality that infants are helpless and rely entirely on the protection of others, this paranoid state of mind is, for them, a wholly realistic reaction to the world.

The second state of mind that Klein identified is less fearful than the first. In this state the infant feels safer and her mind is more relaxed. Even threatening emotions can now be held in mind long enough to be thought about and become meaningful. In this mental state the baby is capable of thinking and learning from her experiences. The ability to hold threatening emotions in mind long enough to be thought about is known as 'containment'. It is, in fact, one of the primary roles that parents perform for their children as they gradually come to terms with what is initially a frightening and incomprehensible world. It is also one of the main roles a psychotherapist performs, by holding a client's terrifying emotions and allowing them to think about them, perhaps for the first time in their lives. Making overwhelming emotion comprehensible is one of the principle means to enable healing and adaptation to the world.

As adults, we continue to experience both the paranoid and relaxed states of mind as part of normal human functioning, switching from one to the other depending on circumstances. As we develop into adults the balance normally shifts, so that the paranoid state that dominates in infancy fades as our minds mature. For some individuals, however, their adult minds never mature beyond a primitive state of paranoia. For such people – those with paranoid personality disorder – the structure of their minds becomes frozen in a perpetual state of emergency, rendering them incapable of normal relaxed thinking.

The mental functioning of those with paranoid personality disorder differs in a number of important ways from the majority population. The first feature of paranoia, as with the other personality disorders we are considering, is its rigidity. A paranoid person holds an extremely fixed preconception that everyone is out to harm them. Holding this suspicion with absolute conviction, they will not be persuaded otherwise. Indeed, anyone who tries to convince them otherwise will not only fail, but will immediately become an object of suspicion themselves.

A second characteristic of paranoid thinking is a narrowness of focus, resulting in extreme attention to detail. People with paranoid personality disorder are not oblivious to the world around them. In fact, they scrutinize the world around them with an intensity of focus that is beyond the ability of most normal people. Nothing out of the ordinary will escape their attention. The difficulty is that their focus of attention is confined to matters that the paranoid person identifies as threatening. As a result, the content of a paranoid person's thoughts is incapable of being modified by the broader context which the person is incapable of registering.

Like those with narcissistic personality disorder, people with paranoid personality disorder are capable of empathy and regard for others. They may not suffer from the cold-bloodedness of the psychopath and under normal circumstances may be less likely to resort to violence or criminality. In situations of civil unrest, however, individuals with paranoid personality disorder play a central role in fomenting hatred against enemies, real and imagined. In doing so, they have paved the way for some of the worst atrocities in history.

How Individual Disorders Become Mass Pathology

People with dangerous personality disorders represent a risk to society when they act alone. This is seen, for example, in the high proportion of homicides that are carried out by psychopaths. A much greater danger arises, however, when those with dangerous personality disorders act together. As we shall explore in later chapters, instances of mass political violence typically occur when psychopaths, narcissists, and paranoids cooperate. In fact, when the ruthlessness of psychopaths combines with the arrogance of narcissists, and the fear mongering of paranoids, society often has little defense.

It is also common for these disorders to co-exist in one

individual. This book will argue that leaders such as Stalin, Mao, Hitler, and Pol Pot suffered from one or more dangerous personality disorders. While there is not universal agreement on this among political psychologists and historians, support for this argument comes from previous studies of these leaders' psychologies. Political scientist Betty Glad concluded that a mixture of psychopathic, narcissistic, and paranoid personality disorders provides the most complete description of the basic character structure of the tyrant, in an analysis that included Hitler and Stalin.[20] In *Hitler: Diagnosis of a Destructive Prophet*, psychiatrist Fritz Redlich reviewed many thousands of pages of documents, including the records of Hitler's attending physicians, and interviewed eyewitnesses to Hitler's behavior, and found clear evidence for severe paranoia and narcissism.[21] Historian Michael Sheng concluded that Mao had narcissistic personality disorder by pointing to evidence for the grandiosity-inferiority complex which is at the core of narcissistic personality disorder. Sheng argued that narcissism was evident in Mao's childhood and predated his rise to power.[22]

The tyrants we will consider each played a central role in directing events which led to the deaths of millions. But they did not act alone. Instead, they were all part of a mass movement comprised of a small percentage of psychologically disordered individuals who were able to co-opt many psychologically normal people to their cause. A key to understanding the danger that people with dangerous personality disorders pose, therefore, is to understand how individual disorders become mass pathology. Two writers in particular can help us understand how this happens. The first is Polish psychologist Andrew Lobaczewski, who was the first to describe how a group of pathological individuals can band together and rise to power. The second is American writer Eric Hoffer, who has vividly described how the psychology of the majority of normal people leaves us vulnerable to becoming enthusiastic participants in the atrocities that pathological groups inevitably commit.

The key point of democracy is the avoidance of dictatorship...the avoidance of a form of rule that is not the rule of law.[23]
Karl Popper

The influence of the minority with dangerous personality disorders, while always present, waxes and wanes as their environment encourages or deters their emergence. In times of war, and the civil unrest that precipitates war, these individuals' personality disorders become an asset, enabling them to emerge and to acquire positions of deadly influence. At such times, as Freud saw clearly, their cruel aggressiveness manifests itself, revealing man as 'a savage beast to whom consideration towards his own kind is something alien.'

Andrew Lobaczewski, a Polish psychologist who lived through Poland's suffering under both Nazi and Soviet occupation during World War Two, was the first person to describe the process through which a pathological minority can come to dominate a nation.[24]

At the level of the individual, Lobaczewski showed that, aside from their destructive behavior which often only emerges later, the most reliable means of recognizing someone with a dangerous personality disorder is through the detrimental effects they have on the ability of psychologically normal people to think. When faced with someone with such a personality disorder, normal people experience confusion. The reason for this lies in the dissonant nature of personality-disordered people's thought processes. In conversation, such individuals will commonly insist on something which is clearly not true, or stridently question the most obvious of facts. These, and other illogical assertions, flow so effortlessly and are held with such self-assured conviction that they can block a normal person's ability to think clearly. Faced with such illogical challenges, most people search for compromise, try to reconcile the illogical assertions made, and end up confused and insecure as a result. People with personality disorders are therefore seen variously as incomprehensible, difficult, ruthless, selfish, but often charming too, 'unique characters' – descriptors that fail to signal the real threat they pose.

At the level of the group, Lobaczewski points to a loss of common sense, a growing collective confusion, and an increasing inability to perceive psychological reality as the first warning signs that a group is beginning to come under the influence of people with personality disorders. As the minority who suffer from psychological deviations take control, the erosion of normal reasoning creates further opportunities for pathological individuals to gain influence. People with a normal sense of psychological reality find themselves in conflict with the newly dominant group and leave, while more individuals with personality disorders are attracted to the group and join. Those who leave are invariably bitter and disillusioned at the group's degeneration and cannot understand what has gone wrong. In practice this phase of the group's deterioration can become brutal – marked either by psychological bullying or by physical violence. Many of the psychologically normal members of the group invariably fall victim to the ruthlessness of the newly dominant members.

Once in control, the group's psychologically deviant leaders apply rigorous procedures for selecting new members. Anyone exhibiting mental independence or obvious psychological normality is excluded. Surrounded by like-minded people and with their power consolidated, issues that are psychologically and morally pathological – such as the use of terror – are openly discussed and become normalized.

The next step is the group's rise to power in society – the stage at which the pathological group comes to dominate the nation. If this occurs through violent revolution, the most violent and ruthless members of the group have the opportunity to demonstrate the effectiveness of their barbarism. Resistance by the normal majority of society is met with ruthless terror. Having seized power, the pathological minority asserts its control through fear, indoctrination, and extermination. Individuals who suffer from personality disorders, and who had hitherto not been involved in the group's rise to power, emerge from within every community to assume positions of responsibility and become indispensable in spreading terror through every village, community, and region of society. The emergence of people with personality disorders across all boundaries of class, nationality, and ethnicity, emboldened by the new circumstances, is crucial in consolidating pathological control. Society quickly becomes stratified on the basis of psychological abnormality and normality, with the small percentage of psychologically deviant individuals holding sway over the normal majority of the population. As we shall see, pathological leaders such as Stalin, Mao, Hitler, and Pol Pot understood this dynamic very well and exploited it to devastating effect.

Pathological groups, being by definition a minority, could not gain power without co-opting large sections of the normal majority. As Lobaczewski highlights, ideology plays a crucial role in co-opting ordinary people to the cause and in helping the pathological group seize control.[25] A compelling ideology plays a powerful role when it resonates both with the mass of psychologically normal people and with the personality-disordered minority. People with personality disorders invariably view the world of ordinary people as oppressive and incomprehensible. Their whole life experience is one of being different from the majority, of feeling wronged and misunderstood, and of being treated unjustly by being denied what they feel is rightly their due. By virtue of their different psychological nature they will inevitably have been hurt by normal society. As we have seen, many may have been physically and emotionally harmed in childhood. An ideology which promises a radical righting of wrongs and the empowerment of the downtrodden, which of course includes a wide range of ideologies from Marxism to Islamism, will appeal to pathological individuals as a means to overcome the limits placed upon them by normal society. In societies where real injustice and oppression exist, such an ideology may also of course appeal to the mass of normal people. Under circumstances of major social injustice and unrest, the rhetoric of psychologically deviant individuals preaching war and revolution and targeting vulnerable scapegoats may easily achieve widespread appeal, even though the ideology resonates with normal and psychologically deviant people for entirely different reasons. Ideology, holding a values-based view of how the world is and how it ought to be is, of course, completely normal and necessary for human progress. The point here is that a given ideology can appeal to people with personality disorders and to people with normal psychology for radically different reasons.

Once the pathological group is in power the ideology's purpose changes dramatically. Then ideology no longer serves as a calling for people to right injustice, and becomes instead a hollow disguise to mask the fact that those in power have no interest in justice for the majority. For the psychological deviants in power, the real agenda is unfettered power for themselves, and the ability to treat normal people with brutality and disdain. Through the use of propaganda and the cult of personality, tyrants attempt to hide from the normal majority the contemptuous attitude toward the official ideology held by the ruling elite themselves. The fact that a powerful ideology inevitably degenerates into hollow rhetoric under a pathological tyranny does not mean, of course, that it did not originally contain elements of truth and value – quite the opposite. It is precisely the value which the normal majority ascribes to an ideology that allows it to act as a disguise for pathological groups in their rise

29

to power and which serves as a justification for their program of evil once in control. Without the masking ideology, nothing would remain except a naked and terrifying moral pathology.

Mass movements can rise and spread without belief in a God, but never without belief in a devil.
Eric Hoffer

The second writer who can help us understand how a minority with dangerous personality disorders can gain influence over an entire society is Eric Hoffer. A self-educated dock laborer, Hoffer's book *The True Believer* is regarded as a classic of political psychology. In it he warns about the danger of mass movements which compel many ordinary people to sacrifice themselves to a 'greater' cause, a process in which destructive charismatic leaders play a central role.

Political scientists describe destructive charismatics as leaders who can inspire great numbers of followers through their strength of personality and their exceptional ability to use rhetoric to influence and persuade others. They inspire loyalty and obedience in their followers who see them as someone who can achieve heroic feats while nurturing them and leading them to a better future. In reality, however, when in power destructive charismatics have no interest in nurturing their followers and are more likely to reduce them to the status of slaves. Although not all charismatic leaders are destructive, as evidenced by towering figures in the history of modern democracy such as Mahatma Gandhi, Martin Luther King, and Nelson Mandela, political scientists have noted a frequent association between charisma and dysfunctional narcissism.[26] This link is evident in the twentieth century's greatest despots, including Stalin, Mao, Hitler, and Pol Pot.

Destructive charismatics, as Hoffer points out, all use the same deceptively simple formula in their efforts to achieve power.

According to Hoffer, every destructive mass movement, be it communism, Nazism, ultra-nationalism, or religious extremism, operates on the following simple dynamic. Every such movement stirs passions within the population based on a widespread hope for change. But between this longing for change and change itself lie 'obstacles' that must be removed. These 'obstacles' – be they capitalists, Jews, foreigners, or infidels – become the focus of intolerance and hatred. Leaders of dangerous mass movements are masters at generating and manipulating the emotions that arise from this deceptively simple process. The success of any mass movement, Hoffer writes, lies in its ability to tap into a widespread desire for change and persuade people to surrender their individuality in pursuit of this 'greater' cause. This task is made easier by the fact that, for most of us, mass movements are powerfully attractive. When we become part of a mass movement, we feel a source of strength greater than anything we can feel as individuals. We cease to be our limited selves and become instead part of something eternal – a party, a religion, a race, a nation. Becoming part of such a movement can make us feel that we have found new life and new meaning.

Identifying with such a group, however, can also detach us from reality. In fact, Hoffer explains, to be effective it is essential for the movement's leadership to detach their followers from reality. 'The effectiveness of a doctrine', Hoffer writes, 'should not be judged by its profundity, sublimity or the validity of the truths it embodies, but by how thoroughly it insulates the individual from his self and the world as it is.'[27] Members of the group must be persuaded to belittle the present and to focus their attention on a promised utopian future. In their searing speeches, the movement's leaders urge their followers to sacrifice their present, transitory selves for eternal, heroic selves and to sacrifice all for the cause. Such thinking is, of course, deeply embedded in many religions.

Successful leaders of mass movements therefore must know

how to generate hope and a passion for change. On the darker side, they must also know how to exploit the powerful emotions that are evoked whenever progress toward the longed-for goal is thwarted or delayed. These leaders know that they can consolidate their power by stoking hatred and paranoia and by directing the masses' hostility toward an unpopular 'enemy'. If such enemies do not exist, they can readily be invented. This dangerous dynamic was captured by Hoffer in his memorable quote: 'Mass movements can rise and spread without belief in a God, but never without belief in a devil.'

Having given up their individual identities to the group in the service of attaining a longed-for future, the members of the movement are now asked to buy into the leader's conviction that success depends on eradicating the 'obstacles' that stand in the way. The deadliness of the movement now hinges on convincing the masses that their opponents are the incarceration of evil and must be crushed. Once the individuals making up the group buy into the leader's paranoia, Hoffer writes, a new sense of freedom awaits:

There is no telling to what extremes of cruelty and ruthlessness a man will go when he is freed from the fears, hesitations, doubts and the vague stirrings of decency that go with individual judgment. When we lose our individual independence in the corporateness of a mass movement, we find a new freedom – freedom to hate, bully, lie, torture, murder and betray without shame and remorse.[28]

In words reminiscent of Auden, Hoffer warns of the consequences that ensue when pathological groups succeed in persuading the masses to join them:

When hopes and dreams are loose in the streets, it is well for the timid to lock doors, shutter windows and lie low until the wrath has passed. For there is often a monstrous incongruity between the hopes, however noble and tender, and the action which follows them. It is as if ivied maidens and garlanded youths were to herald the four horsemen of the apocalypse.[29]

The Mask of Sanity

The influence of psychopaths and people with narcissistic and paranoid personality disorders is seen every day: in the bullying in our schools and workplaces; in the levels of violence against women and children in their homes; in random assault and murder; in street gangs; in corporate fraud and corruption; in international criminal networks; and in decisions made every day by leaders around the world who put their own power ahead of the common good. Their malign influence is also evident in times of war and revolution when they are given free rein to express their destructive natures.

So how has this remarkable fact remained hidden for so long? The answer is that many factors combine to provide an effective camouflage – a mask of sanity – for pathological individuals.

To begin with, science has only recently begun to diagnose and characterize these disorders. Until now the basic scientific knowledge that humanity is divided into a majority with normal psychological functioning and a minority whose psychological deviations make them a threat to peace and reason has simply not been available. This ignorance of the fundamental diversity of human psychologies has, until now, left us unable to diagnose the primary origin of much of the greed and violence that marks our world.

A second factor is that even when armed with this knowledge, recognizing people with dangerous personality disorders can be extremely difficult. It is deeply engrained within us to assume that everyone around us who looks normal is just like us – emotionally, cognitively, and otherwise. When faced with pathological behavior, most normal people tend to search for rational explanations and interpret such behavior in terms of common sense. In addition, much of the behavior of pathological individuals – uncaring, self-centered, aggressive, and arrogant – is behavior of which most people are capable and generally lies within the normal range of human behavior and experience. Unless you are in close contact with someone with a personality disorder for a long enough period of time to recognize the rigidity and extreme nature of their personality, their behavior may easily be dismissed as simply 'difficult'.

Thirdly, although people with these personality disorders have an increased propensity for extreme anti-social behavior, as we have seen, many are perfectly capable of deciding not to act aggressively – for strategic and not principled reasons of course. Even though their personality structure is radically different from that of the majority, people with personality disorders are sane as measured by current legal and psychiatric measures. They show none of the classic symptoms of mental illness. They do not hear voices or suffer from hallucinations. They are not anxious, confused, or driven by overwhelming compulsions. They understand clearly that the law forbids them from committing harm to others, and they understand what the potential consequences are if they are caught. Consequently, if they choose to break the law they normally choose to do so in secret. Few people therefore may ever see the individual's anti-social behavior. This is classically the case, for example, for bullies who are careful not to act aggressively in the presence of superiors. It is also true for the seemingly normal people who shock their neighbors or work colleagues when they are convicted of murder, fraud, or serial sexual abuse.

As Lobaczewski and Hoffer make clear, another disturbing reason why pathological individuals go unrecognized is that they often appeal to psychologically normal people – particularly in times of unrest and insecurity. Freed from anxiety, self-doubt, and guilt, they strike normal people as having qualities they themselves would like to possess. The combination of a powerful mask of ideology, and the potent attraction which pathological individuals hold for many psychologically normal people, means that, tragically, we often willingly place power in their hands.

The rules of ethics which govern the conduct of psychiatrists and psychoanalysts also, paradoxically, prevent a more productive interaction between mental health professionals and political scientists in elucidating the connections between people with dangerous personality disorders and political violence and corporate misconduct. This code of ethics states that it is unethical for a psychiatrist to offer a professional opinion concerning a public figure unless he/she has conducted an examination of that public figure and has been authorized by that person to do so.[30] Although some notable psychiatrists and psychologists have worked within this so-called Goldwater Rule to make invaluable contributions to our understanding of the role of dangerous personality disorders in politics and business, the topic has not yet received the attention it warrants from mainstream psychiatry and psychology.[31] As a result, the concept of personality disorders has so far been applied mainly to understanding individual emotional development and behavior, rather than to understanding the influence of individuals with these disorders upon large groups and societies. The ethnic, religious, and cultural conflicts that are a pervasive feature of contemporary life are unfortunately generally seen as beyond the expertise of most mental health professionals. The election of Donald Trump as President of the United States, though, has sparked a heated debate among mental health professionals and raised public awareness of the issue.

Pathological individuals do not, of course, have a monopoly on violence and greed. Identifying the central perpetrators of mass political violence as being psychologically disordered does not absolve us from confronting the capacity of the majority of psychologically normal human beings for participation in acts of evil. As this book will make clear, under certain circumstances the majority of us are capable of violence and excessive greed. To state that psychologically normal people can and do commit evil is to state the obvious. The numbers clearly show that during genocide and mass killings those with dangerous personality disorders do not work on their own. It is estimated that up to half a million people took part in the killings of the Nazi Holocaust.[32] Up to 150,000 Hutus are thought to have taken part in the Rwandan genocide.[33] These numbers are simply too large for all of the perpetrators to have been people with personality disorders.

Understanding how ordinary people can commit acts of extraordinary violence is therefore an essential part of minimizing violence in the world. We already know some of the factors involved. Economic and social circumstances play a major role in creating the conditions in which ordinary people can engage in violent behavior. People with normal psychology can have a tendency to identify with our own in-group and to see it as superior to other groups, and are sometimes inclined to regard strangers and outsiders with suspicion. Such normal psychological factors can leave ordinary people open to manipulation to support or participate in acts of violence and greed. Experiments such as those conducted by Stanley Milgram and Philip Zimbardo also show the ease with which many ordinary people can be made to act cruelly and oppressively toward others. In Zimbardo's Stanford prison experiment, participants were assigned roles as either guards or prisoners and left largely to their own devices. The sadistic behavior of around one third of the guards was sufficient to traumatize many of the prisoners. In Milgram's experiment, participants were encouraged to administer electric shocks to mock victims in order to punish them for incorrectly answering set questions. Of the 40 people taking part, 26 administered the highest possible voltage despite the apparent suffering they were causing. Recent research by psychologist Nour Kteily and colleagues has also shown that the tendency to dehumanize those of different nationality, religion, gender, sexuality, or ethnicity is widespread within societies and increases in times of actual or perceived threat.[34] Devising more effective means of containing violence and greed will require an understanding both of why a minority of people are prone to extremes of violence and greed due to disorders of personality, and the conditions which encourage ordinary people to act likewise. The fact that ordinary people can kill and steal should not blind us, however, to the leading role which people with psychopathic, narcissistic, and paranoid personality disorders play in the genesis of evil.

The best current estimates are that people with psychopathic personality disorder make up between 0.5 and 1 percent of the general population.[35] People with narcissistic personality disorder make up a similar proportion.[36] The prevalence of paranoid personality disorder has been estimated to be as high as 4.4 percent of the general population.[37] Many possibilities as to the causes of these personality disorders are being investigated, including the effects of drugs and alcohol in adolescence, brain damage caused by difficulties at birth, and genetics. Parenting, as we have seen, is thought to play a crucial role. Given our current state of knowledge, however, all that can be said with certainty is that a combination of genetic and environmental influences is involved. Disturbingly, there is little evidence so far to indicate that dangerous personality disorders are treatable. The absence in psychopathic personalities of something as fundamental as emotional functioning may be as irreversible as the loss of a limb. Similarly, the distortions of cognitive functioning responsible for severe narcissistic or paranoid personality disorders could turn out to be irreparable. The absence of effective treatment may stem from the fact that any such treatment would need to bring about a change in the entire cognitive-emotional structure which shapes the individual's personality and functioning in the world. If personality disorders do indeed prove to be untreatable, the existence of large numbers of potentially violent and irredeemably paranoid and narcissistic individuals in every society on earth poses a challenge to the very basis of established principles of law, criminal justice, and human rights.

However, some psychologists caution against jumping to such a conclusion just yet. They argue that only a few decades ago, few major psychiatric disorders could be treated effectively. Today, a much wider range of effective therapies have been developed, and a much broader variety of disorders have been shown to respond to treatment. Until proven otherwise, some argue, the default assumption should be that individuals with dangerous personality disorders can be effectively treated. To assume otherwise is to risk creating a caste of untreatables, and deprive the world of effective means to address the major problem that people with these disorders represent. Further research on potential treatments is therefore an urgent priority.

In the chapters that follow we will consider the examples of Stalin, Mao, Hitler, and Pol Pot to illustrate the main points made in this chapter. Under the direction of each of these leaders, societies came under the control of severely pathological groups. In each case, the power of the state was weakened by war, economic failure, and widespread poverty. In all of them, a culture of violence developed which was quickly fomented for political gain by a pathological minority. And in all of them, acts of increasing brutality were conducted with the participation of many normal citizens, justified by a powerfully appealing ideology which served to mask the barbarity beneath. Together these examples aim to graphically illustrate one of the book's main arguments, namely that a minority of people with dangerous personality disorders, when the circumstances are right, and when they act together, pose an existential threat to society, including hard-won values and practices such as democracy, human rights, and equality. As the following chapters show, the details of each leader's psychopathology determined the scale of the horrors that unfolded. They also show that, although individuals matter, events such as the Soviet Gulag, Mao's famine, the Holocaust, and the Killing Fields did not occur simply as a result of an individual leader's actions, but were instead due to the complex interactions between psychopathic leaders, wider groups of pathological elites, and mass populations influenced by a mix of propaganda and circumstance.

In his book *Amador*, written to his son, Spanish philosopher Fernando Savater warns Amador that humanity is not a given.[38] We become human, Savater says, in the course of normal development through love and interaction with others. We need to acknowledge the disturbing truth that not everyone becomes fully human. In memory of the millions who have suffered and died at the hands of those with dangerous personality disorders, and in order to avoid the suffering and death of millions more, it is vital that we understand these conditions and their consequences more fully. If we are to have any hope of a more peaceful and humane world, keeping people with these personality disorders out of positions of power, although not sufficient by itself, must be an essential beginning.

2. Stalin and Mao

Totalitarianism

...to preserve a tyranny;...keep down those who are of an aspiring disposition,...take off those who will not submit,...guard against everything that gives rise to high spirits or mutual confidence;... and...endeavour by every means possible to keep all the people strangers to each other.

Aristotle, Politics

Communism was one of the defining features of the twentieth century. The century's Communist leaders – Stalin, Mao, Pol Pot, and many others – headed regimes dedicated, in theory, to achieving a utopian socialist society. In reality all of these leaders wielded power with extreme cruelty, ignoring human rights and the rule of law and ordering the deaths and imprisonment of vast numbers of people. Those unfortunate enough to be living under these regimes, and who had the audacity to question the possibility of attaining communism's utopian vision, were slaughtered in their millions.

The Black Book of Communism, a study by French scholars published in 1997, is the first attempt to chart communism's grim global legacy. It details how communism in its various guises – from Lenin's 1917 Revolution to the Marxist-Leninist regimes of Africa – has been responsible for the deaths of up to 100 million people. Sixty-five million people were killed in China alone; another 20 million in the USSR.[1]

Communism's bloody twentieth-century legacy cannot be understood without recognizing that humanity is divided into a psychologically normal majority and a pathological minority. The discovery of personality disorders, and the way in which psychologically disordered individuals and groups manage to seize and maintain power, allows a true understanding of how communism became such a murderous system. The Communist ideology, with its promise of fairness and equality, provided a powerful vehicle for garnering mass public support, especially among the most destitute and marginalized in society, the working and peasant classes. The violent crises that marked its birth provided psychologically disordered groups with the opportunity to seize power with the appealing but tragically false promise of a better world. Once in power, the revolutionary leaders ruthlessly brought about the segregation of Communist societies into a pathological elite and a terrorized, traumatized, and disarmed psychologically normal majority.

The Soviet Union was the first place in which the circumstances were right for a pathological group to seize power under the banner of communism. Having done so, in the Revolution of 1917, Lenin immediately ordered the creation of penal colonies, the use of indiscriminate punishment, and the deliberate targeting of innocent people for incarceration. The aim, he said, building on the precedent of 'The Terror' during the French Revolution, was to create a culture of fear in which everyone would be afraid and no one would disobey. Lenin's penal colonies would later grow, under Stalin, into one of the largest slave prison systems ever seen. The deliberate and systematic use of propaganda to devalue personal feelings of love, and substitute individual desires and aspirations for devotion to the Party, further eased the way to mass torture, slavery, and murder.

The man who built on Lenin's legacy and plunged the Soviet Union into the depths of inhumanity was Joseph Stalin. He is described by biographer Simon Sebag Montefiore[2] as a man who ruined every relationship and friendship in his life; a convinced Marxist fanatic whose messianic egoism was boundless; and a demanding egoist incapable of giving anyone happiness. He was capable of both reckless outbursts and calculated cunning, was constantly losing his temper, but was also capable of convincing people that there was no one he trusted more. While he seldom attended executions or torture in person, he liked to hear in detail about the suffering of his victims and would shriek with laughter on hearing of a person's last desperate pleas for mercy. His greatest delight, he said, was 'to mark one's enemy, prepare everything, avenge oneself thoroughly and then go to sleep.'[3]

Such descriptions, and Stalin's actions throughout his life, reveal a person with multiple personality disorders, combining psychopathy, pathological narcissism, and paranoid personality disorder. The rise of Stalin and the Bolsheviks to power in the Soviet Union is one terrifying example of how a group of dangerously disordered individuals can facilitate a tyrant's rise and magnify the horrors that such a person can inflict.

The Bolsheviks Seize Power – Revolution and Civil War

In 1917 Russia was in turmoil. Three crises were occurring simultaneously.

World War One was raging, with Russia and its allies France and Britain fighting against the combined forces of Germany and Austria-Hungary. As casualties mounted, the tensions between the working-class Russian soldiers and their upper-class officers were close to breaking point. Lenin and the Bolsheviks captured the mood. They actively repudiated Russia's involvement in the war and agitated for Russia's defeat, which they hoped would act as a trigger for revolution and civil war. Many of the 7 million Russian soldiers involved in the war saw the Bolsheviks as their chance to end the conflict and return home.

A second crisis was unfolding in Russia's cities. Spurred on by the injustices of early capitalism, factory workers in the cities were growing militant. Strikes and factory takeovers escalated as workers campaigned for higher pay and better working conditions. In the countryside, too, there was turmoil. Peasant uprisings against landowners had been going on for years, with sporadic land takeovers and attacks on the manor houses of the rich occurring across the country.

The Russian aristocracy under Tsar Nicholas II, and the deeply unequal society on which it was based, was teetering on the brink even before the outbreak of World War One. The war made change inevitable and exacerbated the ferocity of the upheaval to come.

Tensions came to a head in the Revolution of February 1917, which led to the abdication of the Tsar and the establishment of a provisional government. The Bolshevik leaders, including Lenin and Stalin, were in exile at the time and played no part in the February Revolution. They immediately returned and planned to seize power. In the short few months of its existence, the provisional government successfully survived one coup attempt from the Right before succumbing to the Bolshevik coup in October.

At the time of the 1917 Revolution, Russia's Marxists were deeply divided between the Mensheviks, who were social democratic, and the Bolsheviks, believers in revolution and the 'dictatorship of the proletariat'. In theory, the dictatorship of the proletariat, unlike the 'dictatorship of the bourgeoisie', was meant to stay in place only temporarily, until communism had been achieved and the state itself withered away. As Lenin had hoped, the Bolshevik Revolution quickly led to civil war. In Siberia an anti-Bolshevik government was established by opposition forces, and British troops landed in Arkhangelsk and Murmansk in support of the fledgling opposition regime. Anti-Bolshevik forces were strong too in the Ukraine and Volga regions and in the northwest of Russia.

As the civil war began, Lenin instigated a campaign of violence against his opponents. A settlement had just been reached with Germany to end Russia's participation in World War One, which involved the release of around 2 million German and Austro-Hungarian prisoners of war. Lenin set about putting the empty camps to use, turning them over to a newly-formed secret-police organization, the Cheka, and gave it the power to shoot anyone it saw fit without charges or trial. The first head of the new organization, Felix Dzerzhinsky, was clear on his organization's mission. 'We stand for organized terror – this should be frankly admitted,' he stated bluntly. The Cheka, later renamed the NKVD, and later still the KGB, pioneered the practice of removing gold fillings from the mouths of their victims, decades before the Nazis adopted the practice during the Holocaust.

In the aftermath of the civil war, Russia lay in ruins, traumatized by the scale of the violence. The destruction of World War One, followed immediately by the devastating civil war, resulted in widespread famine. Such was its severity that deaths from starvation and disease exceeded the Russian fatalities from both World War One and the civil war combined. Rather than organizing a humanitarian response, Lenin used the famine as an opportunity to intensify the regime's assault on the peasants' 'backward' way of life. The Russian Orthodox Church, which played a central role in Russia's rural life, was also targeted for annihilation. 'The more representatives of the reactionary clergy and the reactionary bourgeoisie we manage to shoot on this occasion, the better,' Lenin declared.[4]

In the midst of his assault on the starving, however, Lenin suffered a stroke which left him partially paralyzed. A second stroke in March 1923 left him unable to speak. When he died in January 1924, power shifted to the seven members of the Politburo of the Communist Party. Already a powerful symbol of Communist ideology, Lenin was embalmed and interred in the Lenin Mausoleum in Red Square, transformed after death into saintly status.

Stalin's Rise to Power

'How long will you keep killing people?'
'The process will continue as long as is necessary to establish Communist society.'
Exchange between Lady Astor and Stalin, 1931

The inhumanity of Lenin's Bolshevik Party played a central role in enabling Stalin's ascent to power. As Sebag Montefiore states, it would be hard to find a more perfect match between Stalin's pathological personality and the conspiratorial, murderous, and inhuman nature of the Bolshevik leadership.[5] According to Sebag Montefiore, they were a party in which paranoia was considered a virtue; where the perfect party member was someone able to surrender their morality and conscience and unquestioningly accept the party line; and where the torture, murder, and enslavement of millions of fellow citizens was accepted as a legitimate means to further the party's aims.

The contention that the Bolsheviks were a pathologically disordered group is supported by a cursory description of just a few of its leading members:

Leon Trotsky has been described by his biographer Robert Service as a self-righteous, cold-hearted, egocentric who never quite grew up.[6] He demanded that others agree with him, convinced that he was always right. His ugly egotism and overbearing arrogance were accompanied by his fervor for killing on a colossal scale in order to create the utopia of which he dreamed.

Vyacheslav Molotov, for a while Stalin's closest ally, was the Bolsheviks' equivalent of Adolf Eichmann. Molotov oversaw the death squads, the rail transports, and the slave labor camps during the campaign to liquidate the kulaks (rich peasants). He was directly involved in the death, deportation, and imprisonment of between 5 and 7 million people.[7] Cruel, vengeful, boundlessly self-confident, and relentlessly paranoid, he constantly terrorized his subordinates with his blind rages.

Lavrenti Beria, the longest lived and most influential of Stalin's secret police chiefs, oversaw purges in which tens of thousands of people were executed, and controlled the slave labor camps where millions were imprisoned. Beria was a sadistic torturer who insisted that his subordinates take turns in helping him torture his victims. A sexual predator, he regularly walked near his house, pointing out women for his bodyguards to take home for him to rape. Beria's Deputy, Vladimir Dekanozov, was less discreet. He frequently drove around Moscow to find women whom he would rape in his limousine in the presence of his bodyguards.

Genrikh Yagoda was responsible for establishing the slave system of the Gulag. At the execution of Politburo members Zinoviev and Kamenev, he ordered the bullets be extracted from the brains of the dead men for him to keep as mementos. When he himself was later arrested on Stalin's orders, these mementos were found in his apartment along with thousands of pornographic photographs.

On Lenin's death, Stalin therefore found himself surrounded by like-minded deviants in the upper echelons of the Bolsheviks – a situation he revelled in. 'History,' he wrote triumphantly, 'is full of abnormal people.'[8]

At the time of Lenin's death, the Politburo was comprised of seven members: Stalin, Trotsky, Kamenev, Zinoviev, Bukharin, Rykov, and Tomsky. Trotsky appeared to be in the most powerful position to become leader because of his close friendship with Lenin. Zinoviev, Lenin's closest ally during the Revolution, was a close second. Stalin, by contrast, was in the weakest position. He had been damned by Lenin in his final testament, in which Lenin warned against Stalin's thirst for power and suggested he be removed from his position in the Party.

On Lenin's death, Stalin immediately began manoeuvring to succeed him. He arranged Lenin's funeral so quickly that Trotsky, who was in the Caucasus, could not attend, and capitalized on Trotsky's absence by playing a prominent role in the funeral ceremony. Stalin then joined with Kamenev and Zinoviev to attack Trotsky as disloyal to the Revolution. As the power balance shifted within the Politburo, Stalin switched sides to align himself with Bukharin, Rykov, and Tomsky, forcing the removal of Kamenev and Zinoviev from the leadership. Shortly afterwards, he succeeded in having Trotsky expelled from the Party and eventually exiled from the Soviet Union. As Stalin's power grew, Bukharin, Tomsky, and Rykov too all proved no match for Stalin's manoeuvring.

Not content with having established himself as uncontested leader of the Party, Stalin systematically set about having each of his rivals murdered. Sergei Kirov, head of the Leningrad Party and one of Stalin's inner circle, was the first to be assassinated (although historians dispute whether or not Stalin ordered his death). In any case he seized upon the assassination as the pretext for launching a series of show trials in which his former comrades were arrested on trumped-up charges of subversion and disloyalty to the Party, tortured until they publicly confessed to their crimes, and sentenced to death. During the show trials, Stalin personally chose the 'guilty' men, deceived each into believing that their confession would secure leniency in sentencing, and personally signed their death warrants. Of his Politburo comrades at the time of Lenin's death, Stalin murdered them all – all, that is, except Tomsky, who committed suicide in order to escape his impending arrest.

Collectivization and Stalin's First Five-Year Plan (1929–1934)

Once in power, Stalin continued the Party's war against Russia's backwardness. Russia was widely seen as socially backward because over 80 percent of its population were rural peasants, most of whom were illiterate. It was also seen as technologically backward because industrialization in Russia lagged far behind the leading countries of Western Europe.

Stalin had a clear vision of what was needed in order to transform Russia into a powerful, modernized nation. Russia, he said, needed more factories, more railways, more roads, and more technology. It needed a shift of population from the countryside to the new factories in the cities. It needed more education, more skilled workers, and more engineers. In short, Stalin's mission was to bring about the same transformation which capitalism had wrought in the more advanced countries of the West. In the West that transformation had been going on for well over a century. Stalin planned to achieve it in the Soviet Union in less than 10 years.

'One feature of the history of old Russia,' he wrote, 'was the continual beatings she suffered because of her backwardness... We are fifty or a hundred years behind the advanced countries. We must make good this distance in ten years. Either we do it or we shall go under.'[9]

While Stalin's aims may have been laudable, his means of achieving them were deeply psychopathic. In 1929, just 5 years after Lenin's death, Stalin launched his first Five-Year Plan to bring about the rapid industrialization of the USSR. His hugely ambitious plan ordered a 20 percent annual increase in industrial output in each of the 5 years. Such ambitious targets required the discovery and exploitation of Russia's hidden reserves of coal, oil, and, timber and a vast increase in the mining of the nation's resources of gold, nickel, and other minerals. It also required a regular, dependable supply of food from the countryside to feed the growing army of factory workers in Russia's rapidly expanding cities.

However, a dependable supply of food was something that

Russia did not yet have. At the outset of the first Five-Year Plan, a large proportion of Russia's grain came from just a small proportion of farmers, leaving these farmers in a powerful position to dictate food prices. Stalin set out to destroy these rich farmers' hold on supply by forcing tens of thousands into large-scale collective farms and eliminating the richest farmers for good.

The forced collectivization of agriculture began in 1929. Thousands of party officials were sent into villages throughout the Soviet Union, where they recruited poor or greedy peasants to help them drive their better-off neighbors from their homes. The remaining villagers were then intimidated into joining the collective farms and their animals were seized as collective property.

Orlando Figes illustrates how the process worked in practice by telling the story of Nikolai Golovin, one of the more successful farmers in his village of Obukhovo, and his family.[10] The Communist Youth Organization in Obukhovo comprised a dozen teenage thugs with guns, led by 18-year-old Kolia Kuzmin. Kuzmin had spent his childhood on the village streets begging on behalf of his alcoholic father. Empowered to enforce collectivization, Kuzmin turned up at Nikolai's house one evening with his drunken friends. They began shouting abuse before firing on the house. Their shots killed Nikolai's brother who was visiting for the evening.

A few weeks later Kuzmin returned and threatened to murder Nikolai. 'I shall shoot you, just as I murdered your brother, and no one will punish me,' he boasted. Shortly afterwards Kuzmin denounced Nikolai as an opponent of the Revolution, securing his arrest. Nikolai was sentenced to 3 years labor at the Solovetsky Prison Camp in the White Sea. His entire family was then arrested and broken up. His eldest son was sent to work in the Gulag on the White Sea canal; his two brothers were sent into exile; and his wife Yevdokiia and their three youngest children were exiled to Siberia.

Nikolai's daughter Antonina recalls the day of their deportation and the numbing effect that Kuzmin's terror had had on the village. Kuzmin, who had moved into the largest house in the village – the property of another exiled farmer – came to oversee their expulsion:

> I remember the grey wall of silent people who watched us walk towards the cart. No one moved or said anything...No one hugged us, or said a parting word... they just stood there and stared in silence...They were our friends and neighbours – the people I had grown up with. No one approached us. No one said fare well...They were afraid.[11]

As part of the campaign to achieve collectivization, Stalin ordered the 'liquidation' of the kulaks – or rich peasants – as a class. In reality, the term kulak was applied in such an arbitrary way that it could be made to include anyone at all. Those labeled kulaks were often, like Nikolai Golovin, simply the most individualistic and hardworking people in the village.

The viciousness with which the Bolsheviks went about their persecution of the peasants during collectivization has been compared to the Nazis' hatred of the Jews. Vasily Grossman has described the fervor with which the Bolsheviks carried out their task:

> They would threaten people with guns, as if they were under a spell, calling small children 'kulak bastard', screaming 'bloodsuckers!'...the 'kulak' child was loathsome, the young 'kulak' girl was lower than a louse. They looked on the so-called 'kulaks' as cattle, swine, loathsome, repulsive: they had no souls...'[12]

The emergence of thugs such as Kolia Kuzmin in every town

and village across the Soviet Union is an illustration of the process which Lobaczewski highlighted, in which society becomes segregated into a pathological minority (who brutally take control), and the subjugated majority of the psychologically normal population (who are terrorized into submission). The emergence of a small minority of people with dangerous personality disorders in every town and village, who had previously taken no part in the rise of the pathological group to power, is crucial in consolidating that group's dominance over society. While many psychologically normal people may also collaborate with the new regime, either out of choice or fear, people with dangerous personality disorders play a dominant and catalytic role.

Over 10 million 'kulaks' were expelled from their homes and villages between 1929 and 1932. During those years the Soviet countryside was filled with lines stretching as far as the eye could see, growing longer as they passed each successive village. Endless columns marched to railway collection points where they were packed into cattle trucks and transported to the camps of the Gulag or into exile in the empty vastness of the USSR. When peasants resisted by fighting back, the mass deportations simply accelerated.

Those peasants who were left behind found themselves in the new collectivized farms. In the frenzy to feed the growing urban population, the authorities then imposed impossibly high quotas for the delivery of grain to the cities. As a result, insufficient food remained to feed the countryside. The outcome was another famine.

Between 4.6 and 8.5 million people are thought to have died of starvation and disease between 1930 and 1933.[13] Worst affected were the Ukraine, central Volga, Kazakhstan, and the northern Caucasus. In Ukraine this Holodomor, or 'extermination by hunger', is still an intensely emotive issue. Just as Lenin had done in the famine that followed the civil war, Stalin responded not by organizing a humanitarian response, but by stepping up his campaign of terror. As millions died, the Soviet Union continued to export millions of tons of grain, and held millions of tons more in reserve under lock and key.

In one further aspect of the tragedy, millions of children became orphans in the upheaval of collectivization. According to official police figures, almost 850,000 homeless children were rounded up by the police in 1934 and 1935 alone.[14] In response, Stalin introduced a law lowering the age of criminal responsibility to 12, allowing huge numbers of children to be sent as slave labor to the camps of the Gulag. He also issued a decree authorizing the execution of children 12 years and older, partly on the basis that the threat to children's lives would be enough to force their parents to confess to fictitious crimes, thereby securing more slave labor for the Gulag.

The Great Terror and World War Two

The task of the totalitarian police is not to discover crimes, but to be on hand when the government decides to arrest a certain category of the population.
Hannah Arendt

As the campaign for collectivization wound down, Hitler's rise to power heightened Stalin's paranoia. The Nazi occupation of the Rhineland and Japan's occupation of Manchuria on Russia's eastern border convinced Stalin that the USSR was under threat from both east and west. A pact between Germany and Japan in 1936 to oppose international communism further reinforced his fears.

As political psychologists Robert Robins and Jerrold Post describe in their book *Political Paranoia*, it wasn't delusional for Stalin to be thinking that other nations were plotting against the Soviet Union, or to be alert to the possibility that subordinates were plotting to undermine him. But Stalin's pathological paranoia is apparent in his extreme response to these reasonable suspicions – a response that claimed the lives of between 24 and 40 million Soviet citizens.[15]

In preparation for what he saw as inevitable war, Stalin launched a campaign of terror aimed at purging the Soviet Union of anyone who might possibly undermine him or collaborate with the Fascist enemies in the event of German and Japanese invasions. During 1937 and 1938, in what has become known as the Great Terror, over one-and-a-half million people were arrested.[16] These arrests differed markedly from earlier waves of arrest, where less than one in ten of those arrested were executed and the vast majority fed the labor requirements of the Gulag. In the Great Terror more than half of those arrested were shot. In all, almost 700,000 people were executed.

There were many categories of victim. One of the largest categories was those who had just completed their sentences in the Gulag. Fearing that ex-prisoners may bear a grudge against his regime, Stalin thought it better to have them shot. Ethnic minorities within the Soviet Union were also targeted, including Germans, Poles, Chinese, Koreans, and many others. Stalin particularly feared that the Poles living in the western regions of the USSR would side with the Nazis in the impending war. As a result, almost 140,000 Poles living in the western USSR were shot or sent to the Gulag during 1937 and 1938 alone.[17] Party members and the leadership of the military were two other high-profile categories targeted. Almost 120,000 Party members were executed or imprisoned, as was over two-thirds of the Red Army high command.

In 1937 and 1938 Stalin regularly sent orders to the regional bosses of the NKVD listing quotas of those to be arrested in each area of the Soviet Union. The quotas set out the numbers to be put to death and the numbers to be sent to concentration camps. A sample from one surviving list reads:[18]

	Death	Concentration Camp
Azerbaijan SSR	1,500	3,750
Armenian SSR	500	1,000
Belorussian SSR	2,000	10,000
Georgian SSR	2,000	3,000
Kirgiz SSR	250	500
Tadzihk SSR	500	1,300
Turkmen SSR	500	1,500
Uzbek SSR	750	4,000

As Stalin personally prepared the lists, he talked about those whose lives he was taking as if they were old clothes – some should be kept; others should be thrown away. He dismissed the hundreds of thousands of people whose deaths he was ordering saying, 'Who's going to remember all this riffraff in ten or twenty years' time?'[19]

It is now clear that Stalin knew that most of those being executed were entirely innocent. Even so, he believed the massacres were justified. If even 5 percent of those arrested were actual enemies, he said, then 'that would be a good result'. The head of the NKVD passed on Stalin's message to his agents with enthusiasm: If 'an extra thousand people are shot [in an operation], that is not such a big deal.'[20]

During the Great Terror virtually every family in the USSR lost a relative, or knew of someone who had.

War

The Great Terror was followed quickly by Hitler's attack on the Soviet Union in Operation Barbarossa, which marked the escalation of World War Two in Europe – a war fought between two deeply disordered individuals (Stalin and Hitler), leading two ultraviolent pathologically disordered groups (the Bolsheviks and the Nazis).

During the war Stalin continued to exhibit a combination

of psychopathy, malignant narcissism, and paranoia. During the early months of 1941 Stalin received no fewer than 76 separate warnings that Hitler was planning to invade.[21] In a sign of narcissistic overconfidence, he rejected them all. As a consequence of both his narcissism and paranoia, he was loathed to delegate decision-making to others. Throughout the war he took complete control, appointing himself Commissar for Defense, Commander-in-Chief, and Supreme Commander. His mania for control was reflected during his wartime meetings with Churchill and Roosevelt. While the Western leaders brought with them a host of advisors and senior officials in their administrations, Stalin brought only two or three people and did all the negotiating himself.[22]

As the war ended, Stalin demonstrated his paranoia once again. Fearful of potential enemies outside his borders, he demanded that all Soviet citizens in the West (approximately five-and-a-half million people)[23] be returned by the Western allies. This number included captured Soviet POWs, Russians who had been used as forced labor by the Germans, Soviets who had fought alongside the Germans to overthrow Stalin, as well as emigres who had left decades earlier in the aftermath of the 1917 Revolution and who had long since settled in the West. At the Yalta Conference in February 1945, Churchill and Roosevelt agreed to Stalin's demand, and forced repatriations began. People were extradited from Austria, Germany, Italy, France, Denmark, Norway, Sweden, and the United States. Most of those who were forced to return ended up as slave labor in the Gulag. Many committed suicide rather than return.

The post-war repression of Poland, the Ukraine, Czechoslovakia, Bulgaria, Romania, and East Germany, which was to last until 1989, began. Stalin's Gulag immediately expanded into Soviet occupied Europe. Sachsenhausen and Buchenwald, two former Nazi concentration camps, were reopened as Soviet labor camps. Similar camps sprang up across

Eastern Europe. Grandiose projects based on slave labor, similar to Stalin's own, were initiated, such as the Danube to Black Sea Canal in Romania in which 200,000 prisoners are estimated to have died.

Overall almost 27 million people lost their lives in the Soviet Union during the war, two million of whom died in the camps of the Gulag.[24] The Western allies had defeated one pathological murderer with the help of another.

The Death of Stalin

Stalin spent his final years planning yet another wave of mass executions. This time his target was to have been Soviet Jews. In the preceding years, of course, millions of Soviet and eastern European Jews had been murdered by the Nazis. Hundreds of thousands more had fled east for refuge. Now they were in Stalin's sights. Mercifully, in March 1953, Stalin died.

The night before his death he gathered his colleagues around him. 'Some of you think that you can rest on your laurels,' he rasped; 'but you are mistaken.' These words struck terror into the hearts of those surrounding him.

The following morning Stalin did not appear. Those caring for him were afraid to enter his room without being summoned and left it the entire day before entering. There they found him lying on the floor, conscious but unable to speak. Immediately they called Beria.

On seeing his leader struck dumb and partially paralysed, Beria rejoiced. He insisted that on no account should doctors be called for and returned home to sleep his most peaceful sleep in memory.

The following morning, having delayed medical help for almost a day since the stroke, and assured of Stalin's death, Beria finally summoned a doctor. The other potential successors also gathered. Beria, gloating over his impending rise to power, mocked the semi-conscious figure, spewing words of hate at the frail old man. Then suddenly the dying tyrant stirred. Struck with terror, Beria fell to his knees, grasped Stalin's hand and began kissing it frantically.

A few moments later Stalin's breathing grew shallow; he gasped for his last breaths, and died. Beria composed himself, stood up, and spat.[25]

Thousands of miles to the east, in the Gulag city of Magadan, a prisoner, on hearing the news of Stalin's death, greeted a fellow prisoner thus: 'I wish you great joy on this day of resurrection!'[26]

Chairman Mao – Narcissism's Terrifying Vision

...half of China may well have to die.
Mao Zedong

On the 110th anniversary of Mao's birth, a group of dissidents wrote a letter entitled 'An Appeal for the Removal of the Corpse of Mao Zedong from Beijing'. In it they wrote[27], 'Mao instilled in people's minds a philosophy of cruel struggle and revolutionary superstition. Hatred took the place of love and tolerance; the barbarism of 'It is right to rebel!' became the substitute for rationality and love of peace. It elevated and sanctified the view that relations between human beings are best characterized as those between wolves.'

Mao and the Chinese Communist Party, or CCP, provide a second example of how a pathologically disordered group, led by a brutal but charismatic leader, seized control of a society when the conditions were right, and the horrendous consequences that occurred as a result. Like Stalin, Mao exhibited multiple personality disorders, including psychopathy, narcissistic personality disorder, and paranoid personality disorder. The dominant characteristic differed between the two, however, as evidenced by their behaviors and the nature of their regimes. Stalin's character and regime were heavily marked by his severe paranoia, which was given free rein by his absence of conscience. The endless pre-emptive massacres of those Stalin feared would become a threat demonstrate a man living in a continuous state of hyper-attentive fear, constantly conjuring up enemies for annihilation.

With Mao the balance was skewed more heavily toward narcissism than was the case with Stalin. Mao also derived greater personal pleasure from extreme violence. Without doubt Stalin enjoyed the fact that others suffered and died at his hands. Mao, however, found it exhilarating. When he first witnessed torture and murder at the age of 34, Mao reported that he had felt 'a kind of ecstasy never experienced before.'[28] It was an ecstasy he sought to rekindle continuously for the rest of his life. Mao's writings when he was still in his twenties give a chilling insight into the mind of someone with this combination of narcissism, psychopathy, and love of violence. Describing his outlook on morality 3 decades before he rose to power, he wrote:

'I do not agree with the view that to be moral, the motive of one's action has to be benefiting others. Morality does not have to be defined in relation to others...People like me want to... satisfy our hearts to the full and in doing so we automatically have the most valuable moral codes. Of course there are people and objects in the world, but they are all there only for me.'[29]

Alongside the extreme egotism expressed, it is telling that Mao makes no distinction whatsoever between people and things. In the minds of psychopaths, of course, there is no distinction. Mao's musings on his love of violence also reflect his psychopathic inability to conceptualize the suffering that violence inflicts on others. In Mao's disordered mind, extreme violence was simply something to indulge in to satisfy his narcissistic fantasies and relieve the boredom he would suffer in a peaceful world. 'Long-lasting peace is unendurable to human beings,' he wrote. 'When we look at history, we adore the times of [war] when dramas happened one after another... which make reading about them great fun. When we get to periods of peace and prosperity, we are bored...'[30] Mao was incapable of making the distinction between reading about war as an abstract occurrence and actually bringing about the deaths of millions of human beings. Like Stalin, Mao knew that he was different from most people. As a narcissist he believed that he was obviously superior – one of the Great Heroes as he called himself – and someone who should not be bound by the rules which govern lesser human beings. 'Everything outside their nature, such as restrictions and constraints, must be swept away by the great strength in their nature,' he wrote. 'When Great Heroes give full play to their impulses, they are magnificently powerful, stormy and invincible.'[31] Giving full play to his impulses, Mao felt, was his right, regardless of the consequences for others.

Like Stalin, Mao was fully aware that he had an advantage over most of his rivals when it came to brutality. He realized early in his life as a revolutionary that the brutality which he found thrilling – including the torture and execution of others – could be used to subjugate the mass of normal people. Mao made use of this psychopathic advantage by instigating the practice of mass public executions at an early stage of his involvement with the CCP. And after the CCP's victory in 1949, Mao expanded this practice in order to subdue the entire nation. Shortly after achieving power, he ordered a massive wave of public executions right across the country. His intention was to make the witnessing of bloody executions compulsory for a large part of the population –adults and children alike. In Peking alone nearly 3.5 million people attended some 30,000 sentencing rallies at each of which hundreds of people were executed by a shot to the head.[32] Like the visions of the other psychopathic leaders we are considering, Mao's vision for China was a pathological fantasy. His vision was one devoid of beauty and vitality (he ordered the elimination of gardeners and the end of flower-growing); devoid of art and history (he commanded that singers, poets, playwrights, and writers be exiled to the countryside for hard labor, and that China's ancient monuments and temples be razed to the ground); devoid of human feelings (children were taught to denounce their parents and idolize him and the Party); and devoid of individuality (he experimented with eliminating names and had workers issued with numbers to be sewn on their backs).[33]

Devoid of feelings, thoughts, or wills of their own, Mao's aim was to dehumanize China's hundreds of millions of people and turn them into the objects he perceived them to be. Chinese society was to become one vast automaton robotically obeying his every whim. As part of that whim, they would indulge in endless bloodletting to assuage his boredom and continually rekindle the 'kind of ecstasy' which human suffering conjured within him. In 1958, almost a decade after taking power, Mao causally remarked to his inner circle that in order to fulfill his vision for China, 'half of China may well have to die.'[34]

The vision of communism, with its promises of equality, an end to exploitation, and a future society based on justice, provided the propaganda cover that Mao needed to rise to power. But his own vision had little to do with equality and justice, and everything to with ceaseless violence and the subjugation of the Chinese people.

Such a terrifying vision tempts us to label Mao as a monster, as criminally insane, and as a freak of nature whose kind are thankfully as rare as they are extreme. None of these comforting delusions is true. People with dangerous personality disorders are not insane. They do not suffer from hallucinations or any mental illness which clouds their perception of reality. And they are not rare. As Robert Hare has written, they are common enough that we are likely to meet one or two every day during the course of our everyday lives. What makes Mao, Stalin, or any of the other countless tyrants stand out is that they rose to positions of power from where they were able to put their terrifying visions into practice – with fatal consequences for millions of innocent people.

Japan's Occupation of China

Dictatorship is morally wrong because it condemns the citizens of the state – against their better judgment and against their moral convictions – to collaborate with evil if only through their silence... It transforms any attempt to assume one's human responsibility into an attempted suicide.[35]
Karl Popper

War and social instability create the conditions in which psychopathic regimes can rise to power. In Russia, World War One provided the context for the Bolshevik's revolution. In China, it was Japanese invasion and occupation that created the conditions in which Mao and the CCP were able to seize and maintain control.

Japan's Imperial expansion into China under Emperor Hirohito began in 1931 with the invasion of the northeast Chinese state of Manchuria. By this time, senior military figures had already formulated plans for a vast empire that saw all of China becoming a Japanese protectorate. The Japanese army had also established a culture of extreme brutality. To enforce discipline, soldiers were taught to regard orders from their superiors as issuing directly from their Emperor god, to be obeyed on pain of death.[36] When all-out war with China began in 1937, the mass murder of civilians was commonplace, as Imperial soldiers had been drilled to believe that killing an inferior race was in accordance with the will of the divine Emperor.[37] Historian Laurence Rees quotes a member of Japan's secret military police, the Kempeitai: 'We called the Chinese "Chancorro". Chancorro meant below human, like bugs or animals... The Chinese didn't belong to the human race.'[38]

Today, the Rape of Nanjing, a barbaric 3-month long campaign of rape and murder committed against the city's civilian population, is the best known of Japan's war-time atrocities. Between two and three times as many people died in Nanjing as in Hiroshima and Nagasaki combined. But Nanjing was by no means unique. In the city of Suchow, for example, which few people now remember, only 500 people were left out of an original population of 350,000.[39] Around 2.7 million Chinese civilians are estimated to have been murdered in so-called 'sanko' operations[40] in which Japanese forces attempted to eliminate resistance in rural areas. All males between the ages of 15 and 60 were targeted. Villages were burned, grain confiscated, and villagers forcefully resettled. The occupying forces also used Chinese civilians as 'educational tools' to train their soldiers and doctors. James Dawes, in his book *Evil Men*, recounts an interview with Japanese soldier Kaneko-san: 'When they entered a village, they would bring over some villagers... They would tie them all up to trees...And then, "You guys, kill those Chinese civilians", is the order we received. Then we charged in, and aimed for the left part, where the heart is...'[41] The Japanese also used Chinese civilians as 'educational tools' to train their army surgeons. Dawes relates an interview with another Japanese veteran, Yuasa-san. 'When they got there, they were placed opposite four Chinese, and then the jailer, right before our eyes, fired two shots into the stomach of each of the Chinese. And then...we went to different rooms and practised surgery. We practised removing bullets from the bodies. Our orders were to keep them alive until the bullets were removed.'[42]

In what Laurence Rees has called one of the darkest crimes of the twentieth century, the Japanese also used Chinese civilians as human guinea pigs in experiments to perfect biological weapons. Under the command of Shiro Ishii, Japan established a biological warfare research unit, Unit 731, on the outskirts of the Chinese city of Harbin. More than 10,000 people were subjects of biological experiments. The victims were referred to by Ishii and his peers not as people, but as 'maruta', which means logs.[43]

Systematic sexual slavery was another feature of Japanese occupation. Up to 100,000 'comfort women' were forced into sexual slavery across the countries occupied by Japan. These women and girls were subjected to repeated rape at the hands of Japanese soldiers, who referred to them as 'public toilets'.[44]

At noon on 15 August 1945, the Japanese public listened as Hirohito finally declared Japan's surrender on national radio. He was acting, he said, 'to save human civilisation from total extinction' and in doing so was 'paving the way for a grand peace for all the generations to come.' The actions of Hirohito and the Japanese forces in China, however, had created the conditions which would enable the rise of yet another psychopathic leader intent on inflicting violence on the traumatized Chinese people – Mao Zedong.

Mao's Dream, China's Nightmare

On 1 October 1949, Mao climbed the gate of the Forbidden City overlooking Tiananmen Square to proclaim the establishment of the People's Republic of China. After almost 3 decades of struggle against the Nationalist opposition and Japanese occupation, the Chinese Communist Party had finally gained power. Mao's victory marked the high tide of communism in the twentieth century. The Soviet Union, which had been under communist rule since the Bolshevik Revolution of 1917, was now joined by the world's most populous nation. Mao's proclamation doubled in an instant the number of people living under communism.

The CCP immediately faced two daunting challenges: securing their hold on power and repairing a shattered economy. Chang Kai-shek and the Kuomintang, who had fled to Taiwan, still threatened to relaunch the civil war and retake control of China. Huge numbers of former Kuomintang soldiers who had not managed to escape to Taiwan were stranded across the country, hostile to the communist victors. China's economy too was in ruins. It was dominated by agriculture with a poor rural population larger than the total population of Europe. What little modern industry there was had been left in ruins by the retreating Japanese army and the subsequent civil war. The Party chose to use extreme violence to address both of the challenges it faced.

Like the Bolsheviks, the CCP was a party that glorified violence. It was based on an ideology in which the ends justified the cruelest of means. Through successive purges, those dissenting from the Party line were flushed away and replaced by cadres whose greatest asset was their unquestioning obedience to orders from above.

As was the case with Stalin and the Bolsheviks, Mao too was surrounded by abnormal individuals within the leadership of the CCP, again evidenced by a cursory description of just a few of its leading members:

Lin Biao: Lin was one of the CCP's top military leaders during the civil war. He was later instrumental in creating Mao's cult of personality during the Cultural Revolution and was named by Mao as his designated successor. During the civil war, Lin had his army surround the north-eastern city of Changchun and ordered his commanders to 'turn Changchun into a city of death.' By the end of a 5-month siege, the population of the city had been reduced from 500,000 to 170,000 through starvation and disease – a greater massacre of Chinese civilians than that carried out by the Japanese army in the city of Nanjing 2 years earlier. Lin's reasoning was that his opponent, the defending commander General Cheng Tung-kuo, was 'a nice sort of guy' who, unlike him, would eventually be pressurized into surrendering by such massive civilian suffering.

Deng Xiaoping: China's 'paramount leader' after Mao's death, Deng's brutality during the civil war rivalled that of Lin Biao. As the forces under his command swept across southern China, he forcefully conscripted legions of men and women to act as human shields by marching in front of his advancing soldiers.[45] Nationalist soldiers recall being overwhelmed by masses of unarmed civilians as they fired continuously into the oncoming throngs. Deng's viciousness in eliminating alleged enemies of the revolution when the CCP took power was such that even Mao felt it necessary to tell him to tone things down. Deng fully endorsed collectivization and the Great Leap Forward, but pleaded ignorance when tens of millions had died. In 1989, aged 84, he still found dissent intolerable, ordering the June Fourth massacre of unarmed student protesters in Tiananmen Square.

Zhou Enlai: Handsome, suave, and unassuming, Zhou was a master of deception. Chinese Premier from 1949 until his death in 1976, he survived by expressing his eternal deference to Mao. He is described by China scholar Andrew Nathan as a man with a servant mentality, unique in his capacity to endure abasement. Zhou was in charge of extracting food from the countryside during the Great Leap Forward and in doing so played a crucial role in the deaths of tens of millions of people.

Kang Sheng: According to his biographers, Kang played a leading role in transforming China into a 'world of cruelty bereft of almost every trace of human sympathy.'[46] Trained by the KGB in Moscow at the height of Stalin's Great Terror, he was instrumental in eliminating Mao's rivals in the early days of the CCP in Yan'an. Kang was also the chief architect of the methods of mass terror – public humiliation and execution, elimination of the right to individual privacy, and total submission to the Party – that became the key features of life under Mao.

The CCP's brutality became apparent as soon as they came to power. According to historian Frank Dikotter, Mao's first decade in power 'was one of the worst tyrannies in the history of the twentieth century, sending to an early grave at least five million civilians and bringing misery to countless more.'[47] Within that first decade, Mao and the CCP launched waves of terror against farmers, businessmen, those with a university education, suspected enemies within the party, real and suspected saboteurs, and enemies of the revolution. Most of these campaigns of mass murder followed the same carefully calculated ritual. One by one, class enemies would be dragged in front of a baying crowd, where they were mercilessly denounced, mocked, beaten, and killed. Unlike Stalin's reign of terror, in which state security forces carried out the slaughter, Mao insisted that in China nobody could stand on the sidelines. Everyone was to have blood on their hands. In most of these killing sessions civilians were forced to participate in the slaughter of their neighbors, work colleagues, and friends.

From the mid-1950s on, having brutally consolidated control, Mao and the CCP turned their attention to economic development. Responding to a pledge by Khrushchev that the Soviet Union would overtake the United States in 15 years, Mao declared that China would overtake Britain in the same period. Britain, the country in which the Industrial Revolution began, had experienced 200 years of technological change, industrialization, infrastructural development, and scientific and technological progress. Mao proposed to outdo all of that in just 15 years. As with Stalin, Mao's mania for rapid industrialization was to have catastrophic consequences.

Mao's Great Leap Forward to overtake Britain was launched in 1958. In its planning and execution, it directly reflected Mao's pathological personality: a narcissistic vision, a brutally psychopathic means of enacting that vision, and a rigidity of personality that translated into a total inability to change course even when the catastrophic consequences were clear.

By the end of 1958, the whole of the Chinese countryside

had been forcefully collectivized into 26,000 communes. The country now resembled an enormous military camp. All over China peasants were woken at dawn by the sound of a bugle and marched to the fields carrying banners and flags to the sound of marching songs.[48] As in the Soviet Union, collectivization was achieved through the use of violence and coercion, with local thugs playing a central role. As Lobaczewski described, pathologically disordered individuals emerged in every town and village across China rallying to the communist cause, their callousness toward their neighbors now an asset. As one resident of Lijiang recalled: 'All the scamps and the village bullies, who had not done a stroke of honest work in their life, suddenly blossomed forth as the accredited members of the Communist Party, and swaggered with special armbands and badges...'[49] As had occurred in the Soviet Union, Chinese society rapidly segregated into a pathological minority (which brutally took control) and a subjugated majority of psychologically normal people (who were terrorized into submission).

With the communes established, the CCP further tightened its control. Communal canteens were set up at which everyone was obliged to eat. Cooking at home was forbidden and pots and pans were confiscated. In this way, the Party established a monopoly over the food supply. Food now became a powerful weapon to further force the population into submission.

He who does not work shall not eat.
Lenin

The Great Leap Forward was based on the twin objectives of increased agricultural output and increased industrial production.

Mao insisted that he knew best how to achieve both. With regard to agriculture, he ordered Party officials to instigate massive projects to improve the irrigation of land, and ordered farmers to plant seeds closer together and to use more fertilizer. The folly that ensued is hard to exaggerate.

By the beginning of 1958, one in six people in China were engaged in irrigation projects. In Yunnan province party officials claimed that 2.5 million people, one third of the workforce, were digging earth.[50] A massive proportion of the population who were normally engaged in agriculture was therefore diverted away from food production.

Mao also ordered farmers to plant seeds closer together, because '[w]ith company they grow easily, when they grow together they will be more comfortable.' Every conceivable fertilizer was then thrown onto the fields, again in accordance with his instructions. Enormous numbers of houses made of mud and straw were torn down and thrown on the fields as fertilizer, as was seaweed, soot, and garbage salvaged from garbage heaps. The farmers who had worked the land for generations knew, of course, that this was nonsense. They knew that the seeds had no room to grow and were being suffocated by the layers of garbage covering them – but no one dared speak out.

Mao insisted too that he knew best how to increase China's industrial output. His benchmark was steel production. In order to exceed Britain's annual output of steel, he ordered that small furnaces be built in every commune, and that every villager be enlisted to smelt steel. Across the country the sky reflected the glow of hundreds of thousands of brick furnaces, as people drove themselves to exhaustion keeping the furnaces lit day and night.

By 1958, newspapers were boasting about how Mao's utopian food production targets were being exceeded. Once again, almost everyone involved knew that these claims were false, but everyone also knew the consequences of speaking the truth. People who refused to boast of massive increases in output were targeted and beaten. In some villages, leaders of production were hung by their arms and tortured until they reported a sufficiently high production figure. Some died during these public floggings because they didn't exaggerate wildly enough to satisfy their torturers.

In anticipation of the increases in food production that the Great Leap Forward would produce, Mao now went on a shopping spree for foreign technology, purchased mainly from the Soviet Union. The purchases included steel mills, factories, and power stations. The scale of investment was such that branches of Soviet industry had to reorganize their production system to meet Mao's prodigious demands. The food surplus supposedly being created in the countryside was to provide the means to pay off these foreign debts.

By the beginning of 1959, however, it was becoming clear that Mao's innovative farming techniques, allied with the diversion of farm labor to irrigation projects and amateur steel making, was causing an enormous drop in food production. With mass starvation already apparent, some in the Party dared to raise their concerns with him. His response was to act in the only way a pathological narcissist knows how – he punished those who dared challenge him and launched another purge of 'rightists' and 'enemies of the revolution'. Hundreds of thousands of cadres were targeted across the country and replaced by those more willing to unquestioningly follow his orders.

It was at this point that Mao and the Party leaders instigated a policy that was to directly cause the deaths of tens of millions of innocents. Already they had herded people into communes and deprived them of any means of feeding themselves, had diverted millions of farmers from food production, and had issued orders for seed planting and fertilising that were sure to dramatically reduce crop yields.

Now, with food production plummeting and the scale of mass starvation escalating, Mao ordered officials to use any means necessary to extract food from the countryside to pay China's foreign bills and to feed China's cities. Without this order, the victims of Mao's famine would have numbered in the millions. With Mao's order, the final number of dead exceeded 45 million people.[51] Mao justified the mass starvation saying, 'When there is not enough to eat, people starve to death. It is better to let half the people die so that the other half can eat their fill.'

In a policy reminiscent of Hitler's annihilation of 'useless eaters', the Party now banned those too old, ill, or exhausted to work, from attending the canteens and deliberately starved them to death. As one cadre recounted, 'commune members too sick to work were deprived of food – it hastened their deaths.'[52] As starvation caused more and more people to fall ill or be unable to work, the Party barred ever more 'useless eaters' from the canteens. What food was being produced was then forcefully removed and used to feed the cities and to pay down China's debt. A spiral of violence and terror spread across the country as local Party officials stepped up their use of torture and murder to extract the non-existent food surplus. At least 2.5 million people are estimated to have been beaten or tortured to death. Children were among those punished for simply trying to survive. Eye witness accounts tell of one 13-year-old boy being covered in excrement and having bamboo shards hammered under his nails as punishment for digging up roots to eat; of an 8-year-old boy being beaten to death for eating a handful of rice; and of a father being forced to bury his son alive because the starving child stole a handful of grain.[53] The father promptly committed suicide rather than live with what he had been forced to do. Between 1958 and 1962 at least 45 million people were worked, starved, or beaten to death during Mao's Great Famine.[54] This is more deaths than all the trench warfare of World War One, and perhaps as many deaths as happened in all the bombing raids, gas chambers, and atomic bombings of World War Two combined.

While China's rural population starved to death, Mao and the Party leaders continued to eat their fill. Special farms continued to produce high quality food for the leaders, and special shops were kept stocked with scarce goods reserved for their use only. Luxurious villas staffed by chefs and attendants were kept at Mao's beck and call in every province and major city throughout the duration of the famine.

As Frank Dikotter describes, while Mao and his comrades feasted, 'in countless villages, starving children with swollen bellies and pipe-stem limbs, their heavy heads wobbling on thin little necks, were left to die in peasant huts, by empty fields, or along dusty roadsides.'[55] Such images are what the utopian vision of a narcissistic psychopath actually looks like in practice.

All of China was a stage, all the people performers in an extravaganza for Mao.[56]
Mao's doctor, Li Zhisui

As a result of this catastrophe, Mao's power temporarily waned. Deng Xiaoping moved to split up the communes and allow families to set up their own small plots and businesses to grow food and earn money. However, it was not long before Mao moved to reassert his power. Painting Deng's reformist path of economic development as a betrayal of the revolution, Mao launched the Cultural Revolution. From this point until his death, Mao fomented ever more violence until a state of virtual civil war engulfed the country. He mobilized the Red Guards, a mass movement made up largely of students, and encouraged them to attack anyone suspected of being an enemy of the revolution. The greater the violence, Mao exhorted, the better. His *Little Red Book* of quotations formed the centerpiece of a campaign of wanton violence. Mao's rivals in the CPP were targeted, among them Deng who was sent into internal exile. Any form of private enterprise was outlawed. China's education system came to a virtual halt as schools and universities were closed and teachers and intellectuals were denounced, humiliated, and beaten.

Many of China's historical sites and artefacts were destroyed. Reflecting on the deaths he was causing, Mao enthused that 'killing counter-revolutionaries is even more joyful than a good downpour.'[57] By the time of his death in 1976, a further half a million people had been killed and the Cultural Revolution had brought China to the verge of anarchy and economic ruin.

3. Hitler and Pol Pot

April's Folly

Three decades and five thousand miles separate two photographs. The first shows a city in ruins. In the foreground, amidst the rubble, the outlines of what once were buildings are clearly discernible. In the distance lies a vast area of complete desolation, an ominous wasteland devoid even of rubble. Amidst this desolation, nothing remains of the unprepossessing plaza which once served as a gateway to hell. A huge oval, it had been partly surrounded by buildings with roads running into it like streams into a pond. With its perimeter fenced off, there was space enough within for up to 8,000 victims at a time.

The second, more recent, photograph shows a city mysteriously abandoned. Unlike in the first image, every building in this metropolis remains intact; everything appears as it was when the city was suddenly deserted. There are few signs of violence, save the smashed up vehicles that line the streets. The clearest signs of decay are the weeds run amok and the cows that roam the once busy streets. Amidst the stillness, however, one of the city's high schools is still in use. Its three-story buildings surround a grass courtyard, their white paint peeling under the blistering sun. The anguished screams that emanate from the neat rows of classrooms are the only sounds that remained to disturb the deserted city's silence.

These images, of Warsaw and the Umschlagplatz from where 300,000 Jews were deported to the Nazi death camps, and Phnom Penh and the Tuol Sleng torture center, bear silent witness to two more man-made catastrophes of modern times. The depravities they depict, and the millions of inhabitants from each city whose lives were needlessly taken, conjure up images of Armageddon. For the architects of their destruction – Adolf Hitler and Pol Pot

– these are visions of dreams come true.

T.S. Eliot's epic poem *Wasteland* opens with the words 'April is the cruellest month...' And the month of April does contain more than its share of cruel anniversaries. It was the month in which Hitler was born, and the month in which both he and Pol Pot died. It was also a month of tragedy for Warsaw and Phnom Penh. The Warsaw Ghetto Uprising began on 19 April 1943, when the last of Warsaw's Jews chose to fight and die with dignity, rather than submit passively to their fate in the death factory at Treblinka. And on 17 April 1975, Phnom Penh fell to Pol Pot's Khmer Rouge, marking the beginning of Cambodia's descent into the barbarism of the killing fields. April is a month that reminds us that fools shape much of history.

Adolf Hitler, like Pol Pot, Stalin, and Mao, was psychologically disordered. Hitler exhibited psychopathy, and paranoid and narcissistic personality disorders. Psychopathy is characterized by an absence of empathy; narcissistic personality disorder by excessive self-importance, paranoia by the fear of real and imagined enemies. For biographer Ian Kershaw the overriding element in Hitler's character was his boundless egomania.[1] Hitler saw himself as the creator of a new Germanic civilization which would complete 'what Christ began', and 'the greatest German in history'. Had it not been for the war, Hitler said, he would undoubtedly have become 'one of the best architects if not the best architect in Germany.' Like Mao he scorned moral standards, and saw the existence of a conscience as a 'Jewish trait' that should be eradicated. A man who experienced any criticism as intolerable, he revelled in his cruelty. Following a failed assassination attempt in 1944, he had the agonized deaths of the would-be assassins filmed and screened for him to watch over and over again.[2]

Hitler exhibited these features alongside another characteristic aspect of personality disorder – an astonishing rigidity of thinking. Throughout his entire adult life there was no development, no maturing in Hitler's character or beliefs. The arrested development of Hitler's pathological mind helped seal the fate of tens of millions of people and altered the course of history in Europe. To understand how, consider one childhood fantasy and two unalterable convictions. First, the fantasy. The Europe of Hitler's childhood was a continent of great imperial powers, all in permanent rivalry and constant readiness for war. In this land of emperors of seemingly unlimited power, the young Hitler could readily dream of becoming the all-powerful ruler of Europe. This childhood fantasy drove him all his life. His failure to achieve it finally drove him to suicide. While fighting as a soldier in World War One, Hitler was furious at what he viewed as the premature ending of that war. He passionately wished to resume the conflict and secure Germany's victory. In 1926, in *Mein Kampf*, he laid out his plan to do so. France was to be eliminated first; Russia though was to be the main prize. Once conquered it would become 'Germany's India' – a colony which would provide the slave labor and living space that was rightfully due the German race. Britain and the rest of Europe, his plan envisaged, would either actively support the German cause, or stand passively by. Over a decade later, this became Hitler's blueprint for World War Two.

Now consider Hitler's two unalterable convictions, as described by Sebastian Haffner in his study *The Meaning of Hitler*. First, he believed that the laws of nature prescribe that races must fight one another to the death. Any race that defeats another thereby proves its superiority and has a duty to annihilate the vanquished. In order to prepare itself for victory, a nation must purify itself, by eliminating the weak and by selective breeding to improve the strong. 'A state which, in an age of racial poisoning, devotes itself to the cultivation of its best racial elements', Hitler wrote, 'must one day become the master of the earth.' The ultimate end of the struggle between nations is the total victory of a single race. And for Hitler, of course, it was Germany which must 'necessarily gain the position due to it on this earth.' Hitler's second unalterable conviction was that the Jews were spoiling this natural order. They were doing so, Hitler believed, because the Jews did not belong to a single nation. Instead they had spread themselves across many different countries, poisoning racial purity and undermining every nation's ability to fight. Even worse, with their internationalism and pacifism, their global capitalism, and their international communism, the Jews were actively seeking to prevent nations from waging war against one another. Were the Jews to be successful, humanity would no longer be purified by war, with devastating consequences for the fate of the human race. In order to restore the rules of the natural order, all nations must unite against them. The annihilation of the Jews, Hitler believed, was essential for the health of mankind.

Decades later, Hitler's childhood fantasy of becoming European emperor was to serve as his blueprint for World War Two in Europe. His convictions on wars of annihilation as the natural order and the Jews as violators of that order resulted in his successive campaigns of mass murder. First, the mass murder of those who diluted the racial stock of Germany and detracted from the ability of the German race to achieve its rightful victory. Between 1939 and 1941, around 120,000 physically and mentally disabled people – 'useless eaters' as he called them – were systematically murdered. Second, the mass murder of the vanquished. In occupied Poland, the Nazis instigated the extermination of educated Poles and the enslavement of the remaining population. More than 1 million Poles were murdered. The same fate was then visited upon the populations in the captured Soviet territories where an estimated 3.5 million people were executed or deliberately starved to death. Third, the annihilation of the Jews. Around 6 million Jews were murdered during the Holocaust for disrupting what Hitler held to be the primary law of nature, that races must fight one another to the death.

Like Stalin, Hitler was surrounded by deeply disordered individuals within the Nazi Party who helped him create the nightmare that unfolded:

Heinrich Himmler: the second most powerful man in Germany. He was appointed by Hitler as head of the SS in 1929 when the organization totalled 280 men. By the time the Nazis seized power in 1933, the SS comprised more than 52,000 of the most fanatical Nazi elite, devoted to pursuing racial purity and empire. A psychopath who had difficulties relating on an emotional level with other people, Himmler shared Hitler's utopian vision of an Aryan, Jew-free, European empire. It was he whom Hitler charged with the planning and implementation of the 'final solution'. 'Whether other races live in prosperity, or perish, or starve', he told his subordinates, 'only interests me in so far as we need slaves for our culture.'

Joseph Goebbels: Hitler's propaganda chief. It was his role to prepare the German people psychologically, first for war, and then for the Holocaust, by inciting hatred against the regime's enemies, above all the Jews. According to German historian and biographer Peter Longerich, Goebbels 'fulfilled all the essential criteria recognized in current psychoanalytic practice as defining a narcissistically disturbed personality.' A virulent anti-semite and hate-filled sycophant, he was constantly seeking Hitler's favor. On the day after Hitler's suicide, he and his wife killed their six children before taking their own lives.

Reinhard Heydrich: head of the SS security service and the Gestapo. Described by a Swiss diplomat as a 'young evil god of death', Heydrich was Himmler's loyal subordinate and a leading figure in the planning and execution of the Holocaust. Remembered by a senior SS man as 'the most demonic personality in the Nazi leadership', he was someone who 'had to be the first, the best, in everything regardless of the means, whether by deceit, treachery or violence. Untouched by any pangs of conscience and assisted by an ice-cold intellect, he could carry injustice to the point of extreme cruelty.' The Nazi death camps were his legacy. The exterminations conducted there were named 'Aktion Reinhard' in his honor.

Hans Frank: Hitler's personal legal advisor and from 1939 Governor General of occupied Poland. He was depicted by his son as a craven coward and weakling with an instinct for lying and self-aggrandizement who compensated for his weakness with exaggerated brutality. Under his rule Poland effectively disappeared as a nation and became a slave state. A virulent champion of Nazi racist hatred, he ordered the execution of hundreds of thousands of Poles, the enslavement of hundreds of thousands of Polish workers, and the herding of most of Poland's Jews into ghettos as a prelude to their extermination. He proudly proclaimed that his mission was 'to rid Poland of lice and Jews'.

Joseph Mengele: the chief doctor at the Auschwitz concentration camp. He and his staff selected Jews arriving at the camp for labor or extermination and were responsible for conducting vast numbers of brutal and bizarre medical experiments. 'Patients', many of whom were children, were put into pressure chambers, tested with drugs, castrated, frozen to death, and subjected to surgeries performed without anaesthesia, including sex change operations and incestuous impregnations. In one procedure two Gypsy children were sewn together to create Siamese twins; in another chemicals were injected into the eyes of children in an attempt to change their eye color. Reacting to one mother who refused to be separated from her child on arrival in Auschwitz, Mengele drew his gun and shot both the woman and the child. He then ordered everyone from the transport to be gassed by shouting, 'Away with this shit!'

The context within which Hitler and the Nazi's rose to power –

the conducive environment – is, of course, critically important. Imperialism and empire building were the norm, and most European states at that time had overseas empires. For Hitler and Germany to want an empire too was not, at that time, unusual. Concentration camps, genocide, and the mass oppression of 'inferior races', were also all common features of European colonial rule. It is within such a context that Hitler's war of annihilation and the Holocaust unfolded.

The horror of the Holocaust is not that it deviated from human norms; the horror is that it didn't.
Yehuda Bauer

People with dangerous personality disorders, when they work together and when the circumstances are right, pose an existential threat to society. The circumstances in 1930s Weimar Germany played an essential role in enabling Hitler's rise to power. After suffering defeat in World War One, Germany strived to become a democratic state. The Weimar Constitution that governed the republic from 1919 to 1933 was a blueprint for a liberal democracy. The constitution declared Germany to be a parliamentary democracy with a legislature elected under a system of proportional representation and universal suffrage. Turnout in the first elections under the new constitution in 1919 was over 83 percent. The war, however, had left Germany deeply divided, with widespread support for extremist groups on left and right. Elections returned extremist parties, including communists and far-right nationalists, intent on destroying democracy from within. In the political chaos they created, there were 7 elections and 14 different governments in only 13 years.[3] The increase in social instability that followed the Wall Street Crash of October 24 1929 was the tipping point that finally created the conditions conducive to the rise of Hitler and the end of democracy in Germany. In elections held in 1924 the Nazi

Party won just 6.5 percent of the vote. In September 1930, as the economic situation continued to decline, the Nazi vote leapt to 18.3 percent, making them the second largest party in the Reichstag. In 1932, Hitler stood for President and came second to the incumbent, Hindenburg, winning 37 percent of the vote. Prompted by his fear of the growing strength of the Communist Party, Hindenburg made the fateful decision to appoint Hitler as Chancellor of Germany. In February 1933, following a fire in the Reichstag, which he blamed on communists, Hitler persuaded parliamentarians to change the constitution and give him the authority to rule without recourse to parliament. On 23 March 1933, the democratically elected parliament voted itself out of existence.[4]

Following Hitler's appointment as Reich Chancellor, the Nazi Party began to implement their policies to address 'racial poisoning' and cultivate Germany's 'best racial elements'. Under the 'Law on the Restoration of the Professional Civil Service' of 7 April 1933, civil servants of 'non-Aryan origin' were dismissed. In 1935, the Nuremberg Laws banned marriage between Jews, Sinti and Roma, and those of German blood and classed sexual relations with members of these groups as a crime of defiling the race. When Austria was taken over in the Anschluss in March 1938, all anti-Jewish provisions in place in Germany were imposed there too. A Central Office for Jewish Immigration was set up in Vienna to coordinate the forced expulsion of Austria's Jews, with Adolf Eichmann as its director. In November that year, Hitler used the assassination of a German diplomat in Paris by a 17-year-old Polish Jew as the pretext to further escalate anti-Jewish sentiment. On 9 and 10 November, in the incident known as Kristallnacht, Nazis torched synagogues and vandalized Jewish homes. Around 100 Jews were murdered and 30,000 were arrested and detained in concentration camps. Before Kristallnacht the repression of Jews had been mainly non-violent; from then on violence increasingly became the norm. In

January 1939, a Reich Office for Jewish Emigration was set up in Berlin under Reinhard Heydrich, similar to that in Vienna, to coordinate the forced expulsion of Jews from Germany.

When the war started in September 1939, Hitler and the Nazis accelerated their efforts to 'cleanse' German society of 'sub-humans'. Lists of all mentally and physically disabled persons and people with psychological illnesses in mental hospitals and care homes were compiled. After the invasion of Poland, Hitler ordered their systematic murder. His euthanasia decree from 1 September 1939 read:

> Reichsleiter Bouhler and Dr Brandt have the responsibility of increasing the authority of certain doctors to be designated by name so that persons who, according to human judgment, are incurably ill, can, upon a most careful diagnosis of their condition, be granted a mercy death.
> A. Hitler.

By 1941 around 120,000 people had been murdered by injection, medication, and poison gas in care homes and mental hospitals. A Racial Hygiene Institute, set up within the Reich Health Ministry, also compiled lists of the approximately 30,000 Sinti and Roma living in Germany. The initial intention was for them to be isolated in work camps and sterilized so they would die out over time. Instead, over the next 4 years, as the Nazi's murder machine grew ever larger, over 220,000 Sinti and Roma were systematically murdered across Europe.

With the Nazi invasion of Poland, Hitler gained control of the largest Jewish city in Europe. Warsaw, with around 360,000 Jewish residents, was second only to New York in the size of its Jewish population. Immediately life changed. The city's Jews were required to register for forced labor and to wear white arm bands to mark them out. They were banned from public places including restaurants, theatres, and parks, and forbidden to use public transport. Failure to obey these decrees was punishable by death. After 12 months of relative calm, in October 1940, the authorities ordered all Jews to move into a section in the northwest of the city which was to become the Warsaw ghetto. In November the ghetto was sealed off from the rest of Warsaw's population. Walls 11 miles in circumference surrounded the ghetto, topped with glass and barbed wire. Food supplies were intentionally limited to cause mass starvation. During 1942, up to 5,000 people died each month within the ghetto from starvation, disease, and arbitrary execution.

Hitler had four utopian aims in the early months of the war in 1941: a lightening victory that would destroy the Soviet Union within weeks; a Hunger Plan that would starve 30 million people in the occupied eastern territories within months; a 'final solution' that would eliminate European Jews after the war ended; and a Generalplan Ost that over time would turn the western Soviet Union into a racially pure German colony. The Nazi's Hunger Plan, formulated by 23 May 1941, planned to retain some of the conquered Soviet population in the short term to produce food for Germany and the rest of Europe. The remaining 'surplus' urban population of the western Soviet Union, around 30 million people, were to be starved to death in the winter of 1941–1942. The cities were to be destroyed and the terrain returned to natural forest. The entire territory would then be resettled by Germans and transformed into a pre-industrial agricultural lebensraum. Goring was to oversee the short-term starvation and destruction of the Hunger Plan, Himmler the long-term racial colonization.[5] The mass murder of Europe's Jews was, therefore, not the only genocide that the Nazis had planned. Had Hitler defeated the Soviet Union and the Hunger Plan and Generalplan Ost been implemented, the Holocaust would not have been their largest genocide either.

When Hitler's lightening victory did not materialize, however, and it became evident that a protracted war was in prospect, plans shifted, as Timothy Snyder describes, 'from exterminatory colonisation to extermination'.[6] The extermination of the Jews in particular became the priority.[7] Hitler's strategy now was to gain the time needed to carry out his intended mass murder of the Jews, and to hold onto the territories in which he found his victims until this was accomplished.

In January 1942 in Wansee, a suburb of Berlin, the Nazis finalized their plans for the annihilation of all of Europe's Jews – the so called 'final solution'. Located between Berlin and Potsdam, Wansee had been developed in the 1870s as an exclusive residential area for wealthy Berliners, including many rich Jewish families. After 1933, villas belonging to Jews were seized and used by Nazi agencies and high-ranking officials. Joseph Goebbels and Albert Speer were among the leading Nazi figures who lived there. The villa where the Conference took place was a guest house for Reinhard Heydrich, then Head of the Security Police, who chaired the meeting. The 15 participants at the conference represented the Nazi Party, the SS, government ministries, and the occupying administrations in the areas of Eastern Europe under German control. Those present were the senior bureaucrats whose job it was to translate the primary goal of their political superiors – genocide – into administrative action. The minutes of the conference, written by Adolf Eichmann, detail the organization of the 'final solution'. Those present discussed how to organize the rounding up of Jews across Europe, estimated by the Nazi authorities to be around 11 million people; how to organize the mass deportations that were to take place; and how to achieve the industrial scale murder of millions of men, women, and children. For the last 3 years of the war, Jewish families throughout Europe were taken from their homes and hiding places, transported to the east and driven naked into the Nazi death factories.

Among those murdered were four of Freud's sisters: Rosa,

aged 84 years, was murdered in Auschwitz; Marie, aged 82, and Pauline, aged 80, died in the gas chambers in Treblinka; and Adolfine, aged 81, was killed in Theresienstadt.

At the time of the Wansee Conference, the Nazis were already perfecting their means for mass extermination. The liquidation of the Jewish ghetto at Lodz in Poland had just begun, using gas vans as the means of killing. These vans had their exhaust fumes diverted into the sealed rear compartment where the victims were locked. Seven hundred Jews a day were taken from the Lodz ghetto to Chelmo, an extermination camp 40 miles northwest of Lodz, loaded into the vans and driven a short distance to woods where their mass graves awaited. The dead were searched for valuables including gold fillings before being buried by forced Jewish labor. Months later the first of a series of death camps built across Poland opened on 17 March 1942 at Belzec. It was capable of killing 15,000 people a day. A second camp at Sobibor opened in April, with a capacity of 20,000 people a day. A third camp at Treblinka opened on 23 July. Its 30 gas chambers were able to kill 25,000 people a day. In autumn 1942, gas chambers began operating at an existing concentration camp at Majdenek. Gas chambers at a fifth camp at Auschwitz, which was originally a labor camp for Poles and Soviet prisoners of war, came into operation in the spring of 1943. During the 15 months following the first killings at Chelmo, the four camps at Belzec, Sobibor, Treblinka, and Majdenek murdered 2 million people.[8] Deaths at Auschwitz would eventually lie between 1.2 and 1.5 million, of whom around 800,000 were Jews.

Once construction of Treblinka was completed the liquidation of the Warsaw ghetto began. In four phases from July to September 1942, more than 300,000 Jews were forced to the Umschlagplatz deportation point in the ghetto, delivered to Treblinka in crowded freight trains, and herded into the gas chambers. Those not fit to travel were murdered in the streets of the ghetto. To prevent people from realising their fate, the arrival point at Treblinka was disguised as a railway station, complete with made-up train schedules, a fake train-station clock, names of destinations, and a fake ticket window. New arrivals were told that they had stopped at a transit point on the way to Ukraine and needed to shower before receiving work uniforms and new orders. According to the post-war testimony of some SS officers, men were gassed first. Women had their hair cut off, meaning that it took longer to prepare them for the gas chambers than men. Their hair was used in the manufacture of socks and in-soles for the German military. Women and children were forced to wait outside the gas chambers for their turn. They could clearly hear the sounds of suffering from inside and were aware of the fate that awaited them.

In April 1943, German attempts to renew deportations to Treblinka sparked the Warsaw Ghetto Uprising. The revolt was the largest Jewish uprising during the Holocaust. Beginning on 19 April, with minimal arms and training, members of the Jewish resistance – including children – forced the Germans from the ghetto within 4 days. The uneven battle raged for almost a month. After defeating the rebellion, and murdering the remaining survivors, the Germans set fire to the ghetto, and levelled it to the ground because, as Himmler put it, houses that had been lived in by 'sub-humans' could never be suitable for Germans. This is the wasteland in the first photograph referred to earlier.

On 16 May 1943 Hitler received a report that 'Warsaw's Jewish district has ceased to exist.' Treblinka was dismantled during the autumn of 1943. The site was levelled and planted and a farmhouse was built in an attempt to hide the evidence of the genocide.

Hitler was never in any doubt that the world would be grateful. In his bunker in the final days of the war he reiterated his conviction that he was acting for the benefit of all humanity. 'People will be eternally grateful to national Socialism', he said, 'that I have extinguished the Jews in Germany and Central Europe.' When it came to the choice between his narcissistic fantasy of becoming emperor, and his paranoid fantasy of saving mankind from an imaginary enemy, Hitler chose to save mankind. When he realized that Germany might lose, he stuck rigidly to his belief that it was in the interests of humanity that the loser should be annihilated. In November, when the Russian counteroffensive had not yet begun but the German offensive toward Moscow had been halted, Hitler said, 'On this point, too, I am icily cold. If one day the German nation is no longer sufficiently strong or sufficiently ready for sacrifice to stake its own blood for its existence, then let it perish and be annihilated by some other stronger power...In that case I shall shed no tears for the German nation.' True to his word, during the last days of the war he gave orders for anything still standing in Germany to be blown up, and for the German population to be deprived of any means of survival. In Hitler's mind, Germany must be punished through annihilation for having proved incapable of realizing his dream of conquering the world.

Pol Pot's Dream

...the Party leadership must exercise its leading role by use of cutting edge violence...This is the most important factor, the decisive factor, which is the power that drives things forward.
Pol Pot

Thirty years after Hitler's suicide in Berlin, and half a world away, Pol Pot too had a dream. He wished to see an independent Cambodia which was strong enough to defend itself against its larger neighbors, Vietnam and Thailand, and able to resist interference from the great powers, China and the United States. He wished to see his poverty-stricken country develop economically, but he rejected the policies pursued by Soviet communists which placed a priority on technology, factories, and urbanization. Instead, inspired partly by Mao, he saw Cambodia's development as being rooted in the development of agriculture. Pol Pot also wished to see a country of equals – equals that is apart from himself and his ruling elite. He wished to eliminate the huge disparities that existed in wealth and living standards between Cambodia's cities and the rural peasantry. And he believed that he alone had the grand design that would achieve these aims.

Pol Pot's dream, like that of Hitler, soon became the stuff of nightmare. In the 4 years that followed the fall of Phnom Penh to the Khmer Rouge, Cambodia would suffer the loss of the highest proportion of its population at the hands of its own leaders of any country in modern history. Between 1975 and 1979, the Khmer Rouge were responsible for the deaths of between 1.5 and 3 million people. A sizeable minority – perhaps 500,000 people – were deliberately murdered; the rest died of illness, starvation, and exhaustion due to overwork.

Descriptions of Pol Pot typically describe him as a gentle and smiling figure. Kong Duong, who worked with him in the 1980s, after the genocide, recalled that, 'He was very likeable, a really nice person. He was friendly, and everything he said seemed very sensible.' He was also a secretive and reclusive figure. There was no cult of personality surrounding him as there was with Stalin, Mao, and Hitler. However, fellow leader of the Khmer Rouge Ieng Sary recalled the more sinister character that lay beneath this quiet smiling persona: 'His face...was always smooth. He never used bad language. You could not tell from his face what he was feeling. Many people misunderstood that – he would smile his unruffled smile, and then they would be taken away and executed.'[9] His biographer Philip Short describes him as a man whose silences were ominous. Once a grain of suspicion had taken root in his mind, there was no way to stop it growing.[10] Paranoia was undoubtedly the dominant characteristic in Pol

Pot's personality, but pathological narcissism is also clearly evident in his unwavering belief in the correctness of his childishly simplistic vision for Cambodia. Psychopathy too is clear in the inhuman means he pursued to realize his vision.

As was the case with Stalin, Mao, and Hitler, mass violence provided the backdrop against which Pol Pot and the Khmer Rouge rose to power. Three critical factors in particular paved the road to the Cambodian genocide. The first factor was the refusal of Cambodia's ruler, King Sihanouk, to relinquish dictatorial control. Following the end of World War Two, as the era of European colonization came to an end, the young King succeeded against all odds in negotiating independence from the colonial ruler, France. On 9 November 1953, he took the salute at the march past of French and Khmer troops at the Royal Palace, bringing almost a quarter century of French rule to a close. Rather than working to establish a modern democratic state, however, Sihanouk moved to consolidate his own power. In a dramatic bid to avert loss of power in elections, he abdicated his throne, established a new political party, and initiated a campaign of violence and intimidation against his political opponents. As a result, Cambodia became a single-party state, led by a charming, narcissistic, and ruthless autocrat.

The Vietnam War was a second major casual factor. Unlike in Cambodia where independence was granted, France refused to grant Vietnam the same. As the war in Vietnam escalated, US bombing along the Cambodian-Vietnamese border intensified. As a result, the number of Vietnamese communist soldiers seeking sanctuary within Cambodia soared, from 6,000 in 1968 to around 30,000 in 1969. The presence of such huge numbers of Vietnamese forces had a profoundly destabilizing effect, fueling protests by Cambodians demanding an end to the Vietnamese presence. The ultimate effect was a coup which overthrew Sihanouk in 1970 and led directly to Cambodia being dragged into a conflict between the Great Powers. The new government of Lon Nol, which replaced Sihanouk, was pro-US and openly anti-Vietnamese. China and Vietnam responded by backing the opposition forces of the Khmer Rouge, while the US backed Lon Nol. Intensified American bombing aimed at propping up Lon Nol's government destabilized the country further. In total, the US dropped three times more bombs on Cambodia than were dropped on Japan in World War Two, including the atom bombs that were dropped on Hiroshima and Nagasaki. America's bombing campaign left half a million Cambodians dead and fueled recruitment to the Khmer Rouge.

A third pivotal factor was support from China. Crucially, China brokered an alliance between Sihanouk, in exile in Beijing, and the Khmer Rouge. Sihanouk's decision to comply with China's plan acted as an enormous recruitment drive for Pol Pot's fledgling organization. Years later, many Khmer Rouge soldiers would remember joining the organization to fight not for communism but for their king. In 1970, the Khmer Rouge was a paltry force of around 3,000 soldiers. Backed by the military and financial might of China, it rose within 5 years from insignificance to seize control over the entire country. When Lon Nol's government finally fell to Pol Pot's forces, the path to the killing fields was complete.

The Super Great Leap Forward

Eyewitness reports tell of Khmer Rouge soldiers entering Phnom Penh on 17 April 1975, many barely teenagers, to be greeted by people waving white flags and celebrating what they thought would be an end to the war and a return to peace. Almost immediately, however, soldiers began going from house to house ordering people to leave. Some were told that the Americans planned to bomb the city, others that they would be able to return in a just a few days. All were told not to take more than they could carry. Over the following days more than 2.5 million inhabitants of Phnom Penh were forced out of the city on foot. No one was left behind. An estimated 20,000 sick people were evicted from the city's hospitals and forced to drag themselves along as far as they could before collapsing. Others were pushed by relatives as they lay in their sick beds. The evacuation soon became brutal as soldiers began killing at random to propel the slow-moving mass forward. Families were forced to abandon their sick relatives by the roadside as soldiers shot or bludgeoned to death those too weak to walk any further. Twenty thousand people are estimated to have died in the forced evacuation of Phnom Penh. The same pattern was repeated across the country as all the towns and cities in Cambodia were emptied. As columns of people filed through the countryside, they passed through checkpoints where soldiers ordered them to surrender all their possessions to Angkar, a term they had never heard before. Slowly the columns dissipated as people were distributed across the country. The evacuation of Cambodia's towns and cities, and the almost total dispossession of its entire population of their belongings, was achieved within a matter of weeks and with a near-total absence of resistance.

The following month Pol Pot and the leaders of the Khmer Rouge met at the Silver Pagoda inside the Royal Palace in Phnom Penh. Pol Pot had been there before. Born Salath Sar, he was a child of relatively well-off parents who were able to send him to be educated in the capital. Because his aunt and brother both worked in the Royal Court, Sar was a frequent visitor to the Royal Palace as a boy. It was there that he experienced his sexual awakening. At 15, Sar was still young enough to be allowed into the women's quarters, where some of the women would gather round the boy, loosen his baggy trousers and pleasure him. A few years later, in 1949, Sar returned to the Royal Palace to receive a coveted scholarship from the King to travel to study at university in Paris. He was in select company. Less than 250 Cambodians had been educated abroad since the beginning of the century.

At age 24, he set off for France. In Paris he became active in communism and met some of the future leaders of the Khmer Rouge, including Ieng Sary and Rath Samoeun. While there, Sar and his colleagues read Stalin, from whom they learned that communists must be constantly alert against 'political crooks', 'gangsters', and 'agents of foreign spy agencies' and that the only correct response to these 'dregs of the human species' was 'pitiless repression'. They also read Mao, who also emphasized vigilance against communism's enemies and mercilessness toward them. 'Whoever wants to oppose the Communist Party', Sar read, 'must be prepared to be ground into dust.' Sar's views on revolution were shaped not only by Stalin and Mao, but also by his readings on the French Revolution. The French revolutionaries, he learned, had fought not only for France but for all humanity, to deliver people everywhere from the tyranny of their oppressors. The Terror, he read, was an exceptional measure in exceptional times that, although it took many innocent lives, was necessary to secure the Revolution.

Years later, at their meeting in the Silver Pagoda in May 1975, in the midst of the deserted city, the Khmer Rouge leaders congratulated themselves on having achieved the first steps on the road to a communist society. The evacuation of the towns and cities had at a stroke destroyed the capitalist elite and erased the distinction between rich city dwellers and the impoverished rural population. The dispossession of the entire populace had eliminated overnight the system of private property. Buoyed by these successes, the leaders made plans for the next step in what they planned to be the world's most radical revolution – the mobilization of the entire nation to achieve a 'super great leap forward'.[11] The aim of this 'super great leap forward', a phrase borrowed from Mao but going one step further, was to transform Cambodia from a backward agricultural society to a modern one within 5 to 10 years, and from an agricultural base to an industrial one within 15 to 20 years. The vanguard for the revolution was not to be industrial workers, as Marx had envisaged, but the peasantry. The leadership planned to achieve immediately a threefold increase in rice production from 1 ton per hectare to 3 tons per hectare. On land that could be harvested twice, the yield was to increase to 6 or 7 tons. These targets for rice production were set not on the basis of realistically achievable goals, but rather on the leaders' estimates of what was needed to cover the cost of the revolution.[12] The Cambodian revolution was to be exceptional too for the speed at which it would be carried out. National defense, the leaders believed, demanded that such breakneck speed was necessary. Like Stalin, Pol Pot warned, 'enemies attack and torment us. From east and west, they persist in pounding us and worrying us. If we are slow and weak, they will mistreat us.' Massive increases in rice production were therefore needed immediately to gain the revenues required for the massive military build-up required to make Cambodia secure against its foreign enemies.

With this vision guiding them, the leadership issued orders to mobilize the entire population, now remolded as peasants, to the task of rapid agricultural development. Achieving the targets would require opening up new land for cultivation as well as increasing the yields on already cultivated land. This in turn required a massive increase in irrigation and water storage. All of this was to be achieved without mechanization and completely self-sufficiently. Despite shortages of fertilizer, seed, and agricultural tools, the revolution was to be achieved without importing any supplies from abroad.

Pol Pot and the Khmer Rouge leadership did not doubt for one moment that their glorious revolution would transform the country, under their inspired leadership, to be a model for the world. The fact that such a rapid and complete transformation of a society had never taken place before in history did not give them pause for thought. Instead it was seen as adding to the exhilaration of the challenge. So too did their insistence that there was no need to consult the outside world or to rely on foreign technology or know-how. In fact, those who possessed knowledge beyond that of the mostly illiterate peasantry were seen as enemies of the revolution, to be 'ground into dust'. Wearing glasses was declared a sign of bourgeois intellectualism and forbidden. Many who wore glasses were executed, as was anyone who admitted to having an education. April 17 1975 the leadership declared, would be remembered as the day when 'two thousand years of Cambodian history ended' and Cambodia began building a future 'more glorious than Ankor.' They would now lead Cambodia along a road where 'no country in history has ever gone before.'

A Psychopathic Vision of Equality

Their starting point was to reduce the entire Cambodian population to material conditions comparable to those of their forebears centuries earlier. In the 1970s, Cambodian peasants did not live much differently than their ancestors had in the fourteenth century. Reducing the entire population to that level of material subsistence constituted one plank of the Khmer Rouge leadership's vision of equality. But material equality was only one goal of the revolution. Mental equality was another. Khieu Samphan, the public face of the regime, explained what mental equality meant: 'To destroy material private property, the appropriate method was the evacuation of the towns... But spiritual private property is more dangerous, it comprises everything that you think is 'yours'...your parents, your family, your wife...If we can destroy all material and mental private property...people will be equal...if you have nothing – zero for him, zero for you – that is true equality.'[13] This vision of absolute equality was never, of course, meant to include the Khmer Rouge leadership themselves. As they transformed Cambodia into a giant rice field tended by dispossessed, malnourished, and terrorized slaves, the leaders themselves grew fat. Photographs of Pol Pot and fellow leaders Nuon Chea and Khieu Samphan show them all overweight. As one senior official recalled: 'I never ate better in my life.' The rejection of foreign know-how too was never meant to apply to the leadership. Cambodians with medical qualifications were executed as enemies of the revolution, leaving the population to rely only on untrained nurses injecting coconut juice. The top leaders, however, continued to avail of hospital facilities in Phnom Penh and to travel abroad for modern medical care.

As they revelled in comparative luxury, their policies aimed at achieving equality for the masses were brutally enforced. Although families were allowed to continue to exist, their sole function now was to 'beget children for the service of the Party.' Children were forced to call their mothers and fathers aunt and uncle and to call other grown-ups mother and father. Free choice of marriage partner was forbidden. If a man felt a 'sentimental attachment' developing with a woman, he was warned to 'take a collectivist stand and resolve it.' Mothers were instructed not to 'get too entangled' with their children. Mothers would later recall how they could only weep in private over the murders of their husbands and children as to be seen crying in public could result in death. The second in command within the leadership, Nuon Chea, who was also in charge of propaganda, banned words like 'beauty', 'colorful', and 'comfort' from the airwaves of Radio Phnom Penh. As their image of the ideal communist, the Khmer Rouge pointed to the ox. 'You see the ox comrades. Admire him! He eats where we [tell] him to eat...When we tell him to pull the plough, he pulls it. He never thinks of his wife and children.'[14]

For around 2 years after they took power, the leadership kept their identities and that of the Party secret and instructed all Cambodians to believe, obey, and respect Angkar. It was a term totally unknown to Cambodians. The only true freedom, people were taught, lay in following what Angkar says, what it writes, and what it does. Angkar was always right. Questioning Angkar was always wrong and was punishable by death. Asked to describe what Angkar was, one of Pol Pot's former mentors described it as 'an immense apparatus of repression and terror... with a particular stress on its mysterious, terrible and pitiless character. It was...anonymous, omnipresent, omniscient, occult, sowing death and terror in its name.' Under the mysterious control of Angkar, the entire population of Cambodia was put to work planting rice, digging ditches, and building dams and embankments. They were subjected to extreme mental and physical pressure, forced to work long hours of hard labor with little food, and subjected to constant indoctrination to break attachment to 'private mental property'. Communal eating was introduced. Foraging and picking fruit without authorization, which would have helped many avoid starvation, were denounced as anti-revolutionary. As in Mao's China, food was used as a weapon to control the masses by ensuring that people were too weak to rebel or disobey. As in Hitler's Germany, those too weak or ill to work – 'useless eaters' – were denied food and starved to death. In the midst of hunger, fruit that fell to the ground was allowed to rot rather than be eaten by someone who would therefore have more than others. Equality, after all, meant zero for him, zero for you. The scene was set so that within a few short years, millions of Cambodians would die of violence, starvation, illness, and overwork.

Paranoia and Famine

The dynamics followed the same pitiful path as those that caused Mao's Great Famine. Collectivization deprived people of the ability to feed themselves. A high proportion of the population was diverted from food production to work on the massive irrigation schemes that were deemed necessary to convert non-arable land into rice producing fields. The forced resettlement of the population in the countryside with no adequate healthcare meant that not only were material conditions driven down to the subsistence levels of the peasantry, levels of illness and disease also rose to match. Combined with long hours of forced labor, the effect was that between a third and half of the population was sick, chronically undernourished, or both, and in no state to work hard. Given such conditions, harvests inevitably failed. Local cadres, as in Mao's famine in China, had every incentive to exaggerate rice yields and erroneously report that quotas for rice production were being met. To do otherwise risked death. The result was that a substantial proportion of the rice that was being produced was extracted from the countryside for storage in state granaries in the towns, to be used to pay for Cambodia's military build-up. Large parts of the population were left with only starvation rations.

When it became clear toward the end of 1976 that serious food shortages existed in three-quarters of the country's communes, the reaction of Pol Pot and the Khmer Rouge leadership mirrored that of Mao. Given the psychopathic and paranoid nature of the regime, no other response was possible. The food crisis, they concluded, was due to saboteurs and enemies of the revolution. In December 1976, Pol Pot told the Party Central Committee that there was 'a sickness in the Party', and that they should 'locate the ugly microbes' that would otherwise 'rot us from within'. A national network of torture centers and killing fields came into being, designed to do just that. One of these was Tuol Sleng, or S-21, a former high school which became the regime's torture center in Phnom Penh. It was one of around 200 such centers established across Cambodia. Each center had its accompanying execution ground where prisoners were taken after torture and interrogation to be executed. Those interrogated in S-21 were taken to the killing field of Choeung Ek, 10 miles southeast of Phnom Penh, where their throats were slit as they knelt on the edge of pits into which their tortured bodies fell. Their screams were drowned out by the blaring of martial music and the drone of the generator that provided the light for the killers to work by. Kaing Guek Eav, known as Comrade Duch, was the commandant in charge of S-21. He was described by Cambodian author and documentary film maker Rithy Panh as a disturbing man who searched out and seized upon the weakness of others.[15] 'He was an extremely calm man', Panh writes, 'however inhumane his crimes might have been. One could have imagined he'd forgotten them. Or that he hadn't committed them.'[16] Many of the Khmer Rouge guards, torturers, and executioners were children who had been chosen and trained personally by Duch. He chose only illiterate peasant children because they could more easily be persuaded to overcome their reluctance to kill. His training was effective. One child executioner later recalled, 'The prisoners? They were like pieces of wood.' Electrocutions, beatings with cords, making people eat excrement, thrusting needles under fingernails, bloodletting until the prisoner passed away – all of this and more Duch taught his child recruits to inflict on men, women, and children. 'They learned how to guard and interrogate before they learned their alphabet', he boasted. The torturers of S-21 worked from dawn to midnight every day and were never allowed to leave the prison grounds except to travel to Choeung Ek where they would execute their broken 'pieces of wood'. In the first 6 months of 1976, 400 people entered S-21. In the second half of the year, more than 1,000 did. By the spring of 1977, 1,000 people a month were being tortured and murdered there. No one ever came out alive.[17] Years later Rithy Panh asked Duch to name a figure he would like to emulate. His reply: 'Gandhi.'

By August 1977, around 5,000 Party members had been tortured and executed as enemy agents across Cambodia. This 'great victory', Pol Pot declared, had left the Party 'purified and strengthened'. However, during 1978 as the food shortages intensified, so too did Pol Pot's paranoia. In the spring of that year Radio Phnom Penh warned of the necessity of purifying not only the Party, but the masses of the people too. It was the signal for the beginning of the single deadliest period of Khmer Rouge rule. The numbers of civilians killed will never be known with certainty but estimates range between 100,000 and 250,000 men, women, and children killed over the period of just a few months. According to the Cambodian Genocide Program at Yale University, more than 20,000 killing fields sprang up across Cambodia.[18] The numbers of deaths at each of these sites varied from tens to thousands. A hierarchy for mass murder was established, spreading down from the Khmer Rouge leadership to district, local, and village levels. Orders for the elimination of certain groups, such as ethnic minorities, Vietnamese sympathizers, and enemies of the revolution, issued by Pol Pot would be reissued at each level in the hierarchy until they reached the mainly illiterate farmers who did the killing. Refusal to obey resulted in certain death. The killings happened only at night, just after dusk. One of the killers, interviewed decades later by journalist and documentary film maker Thet Sambath, recalled that his hands would ache after slitting so many people's throats, so he would change technique and stab his victims in the neck instead. Another told how after getting home from the killing field he would wash his hands as thoroughly as possible, but to little effect as he could still clearly smell his victims' blood every time he reached to put rice in his mouth. 'At the killing field the stench of blood was terrible', he recalled. 'But we had to get on with it.' Getting on with it, one recalled, entailed slitting the throats of fathers as their children watched and cried out, 'Please don't hit my father. He did nothing wrong. Please let him go free.' The children too would then be killed. Nuon Chea, Brother Number 2 in the leadership, later described how important such massacres of fathers, mothers, and children were for the revolution. 'If we had let them live, the party line would have been hijacked. They were enemies of the people. I have feelings for both the nation and the individual', he stated.

'But I clearly distinguish between them. If we must choose one or the other, I choose the nation. The individual I cast aside.'

As the regime's paranoia and violence spiraled out of control, Pol Pot's public invective against Vietnam increased, culminating in his call for the eradication of the entire Vietnamese nation. 'In terms of numbers', he declared on Radio Phnom Penh, 'each one of us must kill 30 Vietnamese...We need only two million troops to crush the 50 million Vietnamese and we will still have six million Cambodians left.'[19] When Vietnam responded to the mounting threats from Phnom Penh by invading Cambodia on Christmas Day 1978, Pol Pot and the rest of the Khmer Rouge leadership ran away in the face of the Vietnamese advance. Philip Short recounts the words of one woman who survived: 'Didn't they win a glorious victory? But they wouldn't treat people properly, so now they've lost everything. Band of cretins!'[20]

The most profound purpose of history is to reveal something of the nature of humanity in all its extremes.
Ian Mortimer

Poland and Cambodia today are both stained by sites of mass execution – the death camps of Hitler and the Killing Fields of Pol Pot. Seen by us now as places of unspeakable horror, they were viewed in the minds of their psychologically disordered creators as places of purification, places where society was being cleansed of parasites. In Cheong Ek, the killing field outside Phnom Penh, there is a tree against which Pol Pot's teenage executioners would smash the heads of infants before tossing their shattered bodies into a mass grave. In Warsaw, at the Umschlagplatz, German soldiers too murdered children, seizing them by their legs and smashing their heads violently against walls. That is what the cleansing of parasites means to the psychopathic mind.

Today Warsaw and Phnom Penh have become phoenix cities

– bustling capitals risen from the ashes. Warsaw's Old Town Square, the remnants of which are seen in the foreground of the photograph from decades ago, has been painstakingly rebuilt and is lined with bustling cafes once again. The area of complete desolation, seen in the background of the old photograph, was once the Warsaw ghetto. It is now home to the city's premier hotels and nightclubs, and the Stalinesque skyscraper which has become the city's icon. The Umschlagplatz, the point of departure for Treblinka, is now marked by a cold marble monument on a nondescript roadside, its suburban surroundings conveying little of the terror and bloodshed that happened there. Phnom Penh's central Wat Bottom Square too is bustling with life once again. As evening falls, groups gather in front of loudspeakers to meet with friends and to dance. A group of older women move gracefully to the sounds of traditional Khmer songs, another younger group bops along to Asian pop ballads. In yet another group, lines of teenagers, some wearing glasses, can be seen dancing in unison to the sounds of Miley Cyrus, every child moving in perfect synch. Tuol Sleng, now a museum, is hidden among the chaos of Phnom Penh's teaming traffic.

Poland and Cambodia, to different degrees, have both taken steps to defend themselves from ever again falling prey to the predators that ravaged their societies. Since its independence from Soviet influence in 1989, Poland has built institutions of social democracy, including a multiparty system, free elections, a free press, and an independent judiciary. It has joined the European Union and has signed all of the major United Nations and European human rights treaties that protect its citizens from discrimination on the grounds of religion, race, and gender. Cambodia too is making progress, even if it still has much farther to go. Successive elections are widely seen as having been rigged in favor of Prime Minister Hun Sen, who has been in power for almost 4 decades. Despite increased oppression of dissent, ongoing street demonstrations attest to growing civil society demands for greater protection for individual rights and freedoms. Despite the appearances of relative normality, however, the ghosts of Hitler and Pol Pot still stalk the streets of the two nation's capitals. Revellers today in the Panorama Bar on the 40th floor of the Marriott Hotel in Warsaw are largely unaware that they are looking down on the former streets of the ghetto into which more than 300,000 innocents were herded, starved, and bundled off to their deaths. Most of the tourists relaxing in the rooftop bar of the King Grand Hotel on Wat Bottom Square in Phnom Penh are similarly ignorant of the fact that the stunning Royal Palace, whose golden roofs they have come to see, was once the place where Pol Pot masterminded Cambodia's descent into hell. As we have seen, the psychological conditions from which Adolf Hitler and Pol Pot suffered – psychopathy, narcissistic personality disorder, and paranoid personality disorder – are not rare. In peacetime, people with these disorders are restrained by the rule of law and the norms of civilized culture. When societies begin to crumble under the forces of social or economic upheaval, violent conditions provide an outlet for this disordered minority to display their terrifying hidden talents. As society becomes more and more stratified on the basis of psychological deformity, the descent into hell gathers pace.

Were this to happen again, the future camp guards and torturers, the legions of secret police, the designers and builders of the death camps and torture centers, the propagandists, and the cheerleaders of hate, would leave their current jobs as waiters, and doctors, and lawyers, right across Warsaw and Phnom Penh, and assume their new deadly roles. This is not alarmist exaggeration. As Rithy Pahn warns, setting up and running an S-21 is not difficult. More than half of UN member states currently have, or have had in the recent past, prisons resembling S-21.[21] On a sunny April day in either capital, it may be hard to remember atrocities past, but it is also a folly to forget.

The story of Warsaw and Phnom Penh is not simply a tale of two cities. It is potentially the fate of any city on earth.

Lessons from History

[O]ne might well describe the twentieth century as the bloodiest period of utopian political experimentation the world has ever witnessed.[22]
Mark Mitchell

The regimes of Stalin, Mao, Hitler, and Pol Pot demonstrate that people with dangerous personality disorders, when they act together, and when the circumstances are right, pose an existential threat to society.

Each of these leaders clearly displayed traits associated with psychopathy and narcissistic and paranoid personality disorders. These traits included the demand for complete submission on the part of subordinates, relentless paranoia, the blatant dehumanization of opponents, narcissistic rage, tendency to extreme over-optimism verging into fantasy, reckless risk taking, and an inability to change course in the face of disaster. The thesis that each leader suffered from dangerous personality disorders is supported not only by the presence of such traits, but by the extreme nature of these traits and their rigidity over each tyrant's lifetime.

Each leader exhibited further features of note. Charisma was an important factor in enabling each dictator to rise to power. Each gained followers through their strength of personality and their exceptional ability to use rhetoric to influence and persuade others. Stalin, Mao, Hitler, and Pol Pot were also all driven by an utterly simplistic fantasy characterized by a mix of extreme narcissistic, paranoid, and psychopathic elements. These fantasies shaped each of their lives and the regimes they created.[23] And each of these tyrants indulged in narcissistic abuses of power to reshape their environment to support their grandiose visions of themselves. Each used power to eliminate enemies and prevent criticism of their inflated self-image and their prized narcissistic fantasy. And all lived in relative luxury while their countrymen suffered, a reflection of each leader's belief that they were worthy of the exceptions they made for themselves from the hardships they imposed on others; worthy of the lavish lifestyles they led while others starved.

As already stated, however, an explanation of the central role that people with dangerous personality disorders play in political violence cannot be based simply on the personalities of individual leaders. Such an explanation must include all three elements of the 'toxic triangle' of destructive leaders, susceptible followers, and conducive environments.[24]

In terms of susceptible followers, Stalin, Mao, Hitler, and Pol Pot all rose to power not simply as isolated individuals, but as a member of a pathological group which facilitated their rise. Each of these groups – the Bolsheviks, the Chinese Communist Party, the Nazi Party, and the Khmer Rouge – seized power according to the process described by Andrew Lobaczewski. In each case, not only did many of those close to each tyrant also suffer from dangerous personality disorders, but people with such disorders played key roles, right down to the village level, in securing the pathological group's hold on power. In Stalin's USSR, Mao's China, Hitler's Europe, and Pol Pot's Kampuchia, the presence of people with dangerous personality disorders in every town and village, who responded to the opportunities that the pathological group's seizure of power presented to them, resulted, as Lobaczewski described, in the segregation of society into a psychologically disordered minority wielding power over the psychologically normal majority. People with dangerous personality disorders at all levels within these societies actively participated in the destructive leaders' agendas because they shared the leaders' world views, and because they were presented with lucrative opportunities to pursue their own ambitions, regardless of the consequences for others.

This diagnosis of the catalytic role of people with dangerous personality disorders does not, however, allow us to escape the essential role that psychologically normal people also play in acts of mass murder. As already stated, the numbers of people who actively participated in the atrocities perpetrated under the regimes of Stalin, Hitler, Mao, and Pol Pot are simply too large for all of them to have suffered from dangerous personality disorders. People with normal psychology participated in great numbers in the atrocities committed by these regimes. An understanding of mass political violence therefore requires that we acknowledge the fact, which Eric Hoffer stressed, that large numbers of psychologically normal people, when the circumstances dictate, can come to enthusiastically support the inhuman actions of psychologically disordered leaders.

One of the defining features of a person with a dangerous personality disorder is that their psychology is rigidly fixed. Regardless of the environment in which they find themselves, they will respond in the same fixed paranoid, narcissistic, or psychopathic manner. People with normal psychology, on the other hand, are characterized by their ability to think and act differently in different contexts. In times of peace and plenty, most people tend to live with their neighbors in a spirit of community, tolerance, and compromise. In times of threat and scarcity, however, many psychologically normal people can come to feel anger and hatred toward others, and can come to believe that violence and oppression are valid responses to the threats they face. Under such circumstances, psychologically normal people become more willing to accept assertive leaders, and more likely to blatantly dehumanize perceived enemies. As the ethical values of society are corroded, the pathological group can more readily attract adherents from the ranks of the angry and excluded, those alienated from mainstream society, those who endorse anti-social values, and those disillusioned with the failure of the current political regime. Once the pathological group has seized power and the use of violence and oppression has become widespread, the mass of psychologically normal people are gradually forced to conform out of fear for their lives. In this process, of course, context is crucial. In the cases of Stalin, Hitler, Mao, and Pol Pot, the conducive environment included war and social disintegration, the presence of real and perceived threats, and an absence of checks on power.

This description of the process through which society gradually becomes infected with the hatred and brutality characteristic of psychopathy, narcissism, and paranoia provides a coherent and credible explanation of why it is that ordinary human beings so often respond enthusiastically to the siren song of hatred.[25] And it provides a stark warning of how political extremism of any kind, fanned by the hatred of a vengeful minority, can quickly result in outcomes that were previously inconceivable.

4. Democracy as Defense

In our democratic societies a man who believes in democracy seems to us an ordinary man. Maybe even a dull man...Let there be a banality of good, and let it be powerful.
Rithy Panh

This discussion is not about any chance question, but about the way one should live.
Socrates in The Republic

In the tragedies of Stalin's USSR, Mao's China, Hitler's Germany, and Pol Pot's Cambodia a pattern can be discerned.

Prolonged periods of war and social instability, allied to the failures of the existing governing systems to respond adequately, gave rise to extremist groups who sought radical change through organized and targeted violence. From within these groups, ruthless leaders arose driven by dangerous pathological visions. These visions resonated not only with the paranoid, narcissistic, and psychopathic, but found wider appeal because, within the context of the time, paranoid, narcissistic, and psychopathic responses seemed justified, and perhaps even necessary, given how many conceptualized the 'problems' that needed to be faced and solved.

When power fell into the hands of dangerous pathological minorities, the USSR, China, Germany, and Cambodia, then known as Kampuchia, descended into the nightmares that each of their psychopathic leaders willed.

In her book on Stalin's Gulag, Anne Applebaum wrote, 'This...was not written "so that it will not happen again", as the cliche would have it. This...was written because it almost certainly will happen again.'[1] As Applebaum recognizes, the seizure of power by pathologically disordered individuals and groups is not an aberration. Sadly, and regrettably, it has been the norm throughout history.

In the face of the barbarity and oppression of this minority, however, humanity has been engaged in a long and arduous struggle to put in place defenses to protect society from their destructive influence. The history of that struggle is the history of the development of popular, broad-based, and inclusive democracy.

The story of democracy is a familiar one. After its brief flowering in Ancient Greece, democracy almost vanished for over 2,000 years, during which time monarchs, emperors, and sultans ruled the world. There were exceptions to this general rule, most notably in the medieval city states of northern Italy which bequeathed the legacy of civic republicanism. This republican idea – that the highest political ideal is the civic freedom of an independent self-governing people aimed at securing the common good for all its citizens – was to provide a lasting model for Western democracy. After its forceful reappearance in the American and French Revolutions, democracy began its dramatic ascent. During the course of the nineteenth and twentieth centuries, democratic governments grew from a minority to becoming, on paper at least, the predominant form of government. Today, half of the 167 countries in the world are fully or partially democratic.[2]

However, democracy is currently suffering a crisis of legitimacy in its historical homelands of the United States and Europe. In other parts of the world, the term has been stripped of its meaning as dictators use elections to lend credibility and legitimacy to oppressive regimes. Yet despite this deep crisis, the democratic impulse continues to break out around the world. The roll call of mass demonstrations calling for democracy is a long one and reminds us of some of the most hopeful moments in recent history – Solidarity in Poland, Tiananmen Square in China, the Green Revolution in Iran, and the uprisings of the

Arab Spring. These episodes, in which tyrants were overthrown or democrats slaughtered, are among the iconic images of our time. Even as the citizens of the established democracies in Europe and the United States protest against war, inequality, intrusive surveillance, and overly powerful corporations, mass demonstrations continue to erupt around the world against kleptocracy and authoritarian government, as people protest against violence and oppression and call for the public goods that democracy promises – freedom, justice, equality, peace.

In these confusing times, therefore, it is important that we remind ourselves what democracy is and why it matters. And the reason it matters is a simple one – it is all that stands between us and the psychopathic visions of the Stalins, Hitlers, Maos, and Pol Pots who live among us still.

Democracy as a System of Defenses

Democratic Government

The foundations of our modern system of democracy were first put in place in ancient Athens. Athenian society, however, was never fully democratic in the way that we would understand a democratic society today. Slavery remained widespread; women were never allowed to participate in political affairs; and the elite who were eligible to take part in democratic decision-making made up less than 10 percent of the entire population, as only property owners could take part in politics. Despite these shortcomings, the Athenians established some of the fundamental principles of democratic government.

The citizen Assembly, which passed new laws and made all major political decisions, was at the center of the Athenian system. All eligible citizens had a right to attend the Assembly, to address it themselves, and to vote on all proposals that came before it. Citizens could also stand for election to the Council, the administrative body that organized the Assembly. The Law

Courts too were run on a democratic basis. Juries drawn from panels of citizens decided every significant case brought to trial in the city state.

The Athenians were proud of their democracy and believed passionately in the benefits it brought. They believed, first and foremost, that allowing citizens to participate in politics brought social and political stability. In any political system, people will necessarily disagree about what laws they should live under and what decisions their political leaders should make. Yet every citizen is bound by those laws and those decisions, whether they agree with them or not. If conflict is to be avoided, a mechanism is therefore needed in which everyone agrees to abide by decisions made, regardless of whether they personally agree or disagree.[3] Democracy was the mechanism the Athenians devised to resolve this dilemma. For them, democracy was primarily a means of making political decisions that avoided violent conflict. Or, to put it another way, democracy is a way to non-violently disagree. This principle remains valid today. In a democracy, the legitimacy of decisions arises not primarily from the correctness of any particular decision, but from the fact that the decision has been reached through a democratic procedure in which every citizen has an equal right to participate and where violence or the threat of violence is absent. At the heart of that democratic procedure lies the basic principle of equal citizenship: 'each to count for one, none for more than one'. Such legitimacy means that all citizens must renounce recourse to non-democratic means if a particular decision does not go their way. For citizens in a democracy, in Ancient Athens and in democracies today, recourse to force is not an option in the face of defeat.

The Athenians also believed that not only was the democratic process more likely to provide stability, it was also more likely to produce decisions that were right. This is because democratic decision-making allows different sides of the argument, and different perspectives from within society, to be presented and debated. Such a process is more likely to result in fairer and more informed decisions than decisions made by a single ruler or ruling elite. A later democratic thinker and politician, John Stuart Mill, described this in the nineteenth century as 'the collision theory of the truth', an implication of which is that even deliberate falsehoods should be allowed to be debated so they can be defeated in the democratic contest. The claim here is not that democracy always gets the answer right, of course, but that it is more likely to do so than other forms of government.[4] Democracy is also more likely to result in a more just and inclusive conception of the common good, which is of crucial importance when it comes to democracy's role in protecting society against pathological leaders. Because of its inclusive and deliberative nature, democracy, as Aristotle argued, can act as a vital defense against all-powerful individuals or elites imposing their malevolent and dangerous visions on society.

When Athenian democracy succumbed to foreign invasion, it took over 2,000 years for democracy to fully re-emerge, in the Italian city states in the fifteenth century, in the 'Glorious Revolution' in England in the seventeenth century, in the wake of the American and French Revolutions in the eighteenth century, and in the mass democratic movements associated with nationalism in Europe in the nineteenth century. During that long, protracted struggle, a second critical building block in our modern democratic system was slowly being built, namely the rule of law.

The Rule of Law

Of all the pillars in our modern system of democracy, none has had as great an impact on human wellbeing as the development of the rule of law. The rule of law reduces violence, provides a means of holding leaders to account, forces a degree of rationality into political decision-making, and offers protection for citizens against the arbitrary actions of their rulers. A central pillar of the rule of law in a democratic polity is that every citizen is equal before the law and no citizen is above or beyond the law's reach, regardless of rank, wealth, or status.

The dramatic impact of the rule of law is evident in the fact that levels of violence in societies worldwide have fallen dramatically since the time of the ancient world. As psychologist Steven Pinker has documented, around 15 percent of people, on average, died violent deaths in pre-civilization societies. By comparison, the death rate from violence in the twentieth century was around 3 percent.[5] As Pinker points out, changing circumstances rather than fundamental changes in human nature have been responsible for this remarkable reduction in violence. While many factors have contributed to this change, including economic and social development, the increased use of reason in human affairs, and the rise of mass education, the most decisive influences have been the gradual development of democracy and the rule of law. The invention of government with the power to enforce laws, however, addressed one problem – violence between citizens – and created another, namely the use of violence by the state against citizens. For most of history, after all, civilization has meant tyranny, colonization, imperialism, and dispossession. For democracy to act as a defense against pathological elites, institutions and practices needed to be developed through which the rule of law applies not only to citizens, but to rulers as well.

Former British Lord Chief Justice Tom Bingham, in his book *The Rule of Law*, sets out four historical landmarks in the development of such institutions and practices.[6] The first landmark moment was the signing of the Magna Carta between King John of England and a group of rebel barons in 1215. With its signing, the principle was established that even a supreme leader must be bound by certain laws.

Bingham's second landmark moment was the development of the right of Habeas Corpus. This established the right of anyone who was to be imprisoned to be brought before an impartial court within a short period of time to determine whether their imprisonment was justified. Bingham describes Habeas Corpus as 'the most effective remedy against executive lawlessness that the world has ever seen.'[7] The effect of its absence can be seen in many parts of the world today, where it is the norm for those arrested to languish in prison for years without ever being brought to trial.

The third and fourth of Bingham's major landmarks are the abolition of the use of torture, and the development of fundamental principles to which judges should adhere to ensure a fair trial. The use of torture as a means of proving the guilt of the accused was first rejected in England in the late fifteenth century. It was rejected on three grounds. First, that the practice was unjustly cruel when applied to someone who had not yet been found guilty of any crime. Second, that the evidence so procured was profoundly unreliable. And third, that the practice degraded all those involved. The principles to which judges should adhere were first written in 1670 by Sir Matthew Hale, then Chief Justice in England. They included the rule, 'That I be not biased with compassion towards the poor, or favor towards the rich.' In other words, there should not be one law for the rich and another for the poor. Every citizen is equal before the law and no citizen is above or beyond the law's reach.

Taken together the establishment of such codes and practices, which bind rulers as well as citizens to certain moral standards of behavior, came to provide a vital defense against the arbitrary dictates of those in power. When democracy re-emerged in the wake of the American Revolution, the rule of law was a central pillar in the democratic system of government that America's Founding Fathers pieced together.

Constitutional Democracy

According to the historian Roger Osborne, the American

Revolution was the single most decisive event in the history of democracy. Within the first 70 years of the new United States of America's existence, every white adult male had the right to vote in state and federal elections, almost every important public official was elected, a series of national and state institutions had been set up to protect citizens from the power of the state and from the tyranny of the majority, political parties had been established that transferred power peacefully after elections, and a culture of mass participation in politics had emerged.[8]

No-one could have known at the time, of course, that subsequent events would propel this infant nation to global superpower status, and that democracy would become the preeminent form of government that it is today. When representatives of Britain's 13 American colonies drafted and signed the American Declaration of Independence in July 1776, they could not have known the global import of their actions. The Declaration of Independence, of course, provided the inspiration for the Revolution, with its bold assertion that all men are created equal and endowed by their Creator with the inalienable rights of life, liberty, and the pursuit of happiness. But it was the drafting of the United States Constitution and the Bill of Rights, and the design of the new form of government, that were to have the more profound and lasting consequences. Five years after independence, a Congressional Convention met to draft the constitution for the new nation. In the words of future Secretary of State John Jay, Americans became 'the first people...with an opportunity of deliberating upon and choosing forms of government under which they should live.'[9] The task they faced was no less than how to design an effective system of government that could replace tyranny and protect the majority of citizens from oppression. Democracy lay at the heart of the system the American Founding Fathers devised to do so. The new system was not to be the direct system of democracy that the ancient Athenians had used. Instead, the American system was to be based on the idea of representative democracy. Rather than every citizen having the right to attend and vote in the national assembly, as was the case in Ancient Athens, US citizens would elect representatives who would attend the legislature and act on their behalf.

To prevent the government from becoming too powerful, the legislature would be comprised of two national legislative assemblies, the House of Representatives and the Senate. A President, also elected by the people, would lead the executive arm of government. All elected representatives would serve for fixed terms and could be removed by the people at elections to be held at fixed time periods. Crucially, elected representatives would be forced to operate within a precisely defined framework of law, which was laid down in the constitution, the most important element of which was 'separation of powers'. An independent judiciary would act as a check on the behavior of the President and the Legislature. And a Supreme Court would be established tasked with defending not the government, but the constitution. To further ensure the protection of citizens from possible oppression by their elected government, protections for citizens' rights, including freedom of speech, freedom of the press, the right to trial by jury, and freedom of religion, were written into the constitution.

Through this extraordinary innovation in governance, the Founding Fathers found a way to take the fundamental principles of democracy established in Ancient Greece and create a system of government that could apply these principles to nation states comprising millions of citizens. They had created 'mass democracy', a form of democratic government for mass societies. This new form of government – representative democracy based on the rule of law, and a written constitution which provides protection for individual rights – has proven to be the most effective means of protecting citizens from violence and oppression since the invention of the state itself.

Prohibition on State-Sponsored Ideology

Remarkable as this new system of democracy was, US society at the time of independence still retained some of the more horrendous practices of ancient times. Slavery was widespread, women were excluded from political participation, and a genocidal war was being waged against the Native American population. Despite its undoubted advances, what the new American democracy clearly did not do was to guarantee equality of citizenship to all. Citizenship, that is membership of society, is the first issue any democratic political system distributes, and it clearly does not always do so equally.

A more radical assertion of the essential equality of all human beings was the central thrust of the revolution that soon erupted across the Atlantic in France. The French Revolution swept away the system of Monarchy, Church, and aristocracy which had governed France for centuries. In its place the revolutionaries envisaged a more just and fair society in which every citizen possessed equal rights that the state was obliged to uphold. Their radical vision, set out in *The Declaration of the Rights of Man and of the Citizen*, asserted that all 'men' are born and remain free and equal in rights, and that the aim of all political association is 'the preservation of the natural and imprescriptible rights of man.' The failure of the Revolution however – at least in the short term – meant that this principle was not established in practice at that time. In fact, it was not until after World War Two and the Holocaust that the principle that all human beings have fundamental rights that must be protected in law and upheld by the state began to become a reality.

One major factor in the failure of the French Revolution was the revolutionary government's campaign to destroy the power of the Catholic Church in France. The new government launched a nationwide campaign of terror in which thousands of priests and nuns were arrested, tortured, and murdered. The spirit of this anti-clericalism, and its link to anti-monarchism, can be seen in the infamous quote from the French philosopher Denis Diderot who stated, 'Mankind shall not be free until the last king is strangled with the entrails of the last priest.' The opposition of French peasants to their new government's attack on their religion, however, contributed significantly to the spiral of chaos and bloodshed which led ultimately to Napoleon's seizure of power and the establishment of his dictatorship.

In the new United States, a very different and peaceful accommodation was reached between religion and the state. It was an accommodation that was based on another fundamental principle of modern democracy, the principle of 'liberal individualism'. Liberal individualism holds that the proper role of the state is to leave citizens free to choose how to live, as long as their choices do not infringe upon the rights of others.[10] The state must therefore refrain from imposing its view on citizens as to how they should live their lives. Based on this liberal principle, the American Revolution made a radical break with accepted norms by establishing a clear separation between church and state. In doing so, the aim was not to eradicate religion, as was being brutally attempted in France. Instead, the aim was to separate church and state so as to allow freedom of worship for all, regardless of religious affiliation. The Bill of Rights which was incorporated into the United States Constitution stated that, 'Congress shall make no law respecting an establishment of religion, or prohibiting the free exercise thereof.' Under the constitution, the new United States government was prohibited by law from establishing a national religion or giving preferential treatment to one religion over another. Religion was viewed as a private matter of conscience, not a public political matter.

The principle of liberal individualism upon which the separation of church and state was based is of profound importance not only for social and political stability, but also for the protection of individual rights and freedoms. The separation of church and state deprives religious zealots of the ability to use the power of the state to enforce any particular religious dogma upon the entire population. But the principle of liberal individualism has a much broader application. The enforcement by the state of political doctrines such as extreme nationalism, communism, and National Socialism all had disastrous consequences during the twentieth century. The prohibition on the state from imposing its view on society therefore serves as a crucial defense against any government that seeks to extinguish individual freedoms in pursuit of not only religious, but also secular, utopian, or as is more likely, dystopian, visions.

Social Democracy

Like pure democracy, undiluted capitalism is intolerable.
Wilhelm Ropke

The final pillars in our modern system of democracy emerged from the catastrophes of world war and genocide. These building blocks are social democracy and the legal protection of individual human rights.

In the period between the American Revolution and the outbreak of World War One, as societies across Europe were transformed by the Industrial Revolution, Europe's monarchies refused to adapt. As capitalism changed European societies beyond recognition, the refusal of ruling elites to compromise, alongside clashing imperial-colonial interests between elites within the 'Great Powers', led to the build-up of tensions which erupted with catastrophic consequences in the Russian Revolution and World War One.

The Great War left Europe in ruins and led to the rise of the United States as a global economic superpower. Throughout the 1920s and 1930s, new technologies fueled economic growth as never before, but they also radically impacted upon people's lives. In 1914 about one-third of workers in the average industrialized country were farmers; by the beginning of World War Two, this proportion had been halved as factory jobs rapidly replaced agricultural jobs.[11] Many of the new technologies, such as cars and aircraft, also required companies on a scale that had not previously existed. These new large-scale corporations squeezed many small firms out of business. As many farmers and small businessmen lost their jobs, disaffection with capitalism grew. By 1935 these two groups, along with white-collar workers, represented two-thirds of the membership of the Nazi Party in Germany.[12]

The Great Depression plunged Europe further into crisis. The Wall Street Crash of Black Tuesday, 1929, resulted in spiraling unemployment and a virtual shut-down of the world economy. World trade plummeted and a wave of hyperinflation wiped out the savings and assets of millions. Still paying reparations from World War One, Germany was particularly badly hit. In the absence of unemployment benefits or other forms of social security, many people were left destitute. Eventually, as the social and political crisis spiraled out of control, Germany, as we have seen, turned to Hitler for salvation.

At the height of World War Two, the Nazis controlled most of Western Europe, while large parts of Eastern Europe lay under Soviet occupation. Millions were being deported to their deaths either in Hitler's concentration camps or in the slave camps of Stalin's Gulag. Europe's political systems had failed utterly to protect its citizens against the rise of dangerously psychologically disordered groups, and it was paying a horrendous price.

When the war finally ended, and Nazism had been defeated, the countries of Western Europe sought to draw lessons from two world wars, to construct a new social and political order. The wars had clearly shown that capitalism creates losers as well as winners and that the resulting social disintegration provides an opportunity for pathological groups to rise to power. The injustices of capitalism – gross inequality, social divisions, and widespread impoverishment – had contributed to the rise of Nazism and the outbreak of war. In the light of this devastating experience, European leaders now viewed unregulated capitalism as dangerous. The lesson that emerged from the ashes of Europe was that a new model of democracy, based on a new accommodation between capitalism and democracy, was needed if European civilization was to be restored.

This new European model of social democracy had begun to emerge even before Hitler began to terrorize the continent. During the Great Depression, social democrats in Scandinavia had already developed the type of intervention that was needed to make capitalism work for the common good.[13] During the 1930s, the Swedish Social Democrats implemented a major program to reduce unemployment. In neighboring Denmark, the Danish Social Democrats pioneered widespread social security and free primary education. In Norway, the Labor Party enacted similar measures to protect citizens against capitalism's excesses. When World War Two ended, the principles of social democracy pioneered in Scandinavia were adopted across the continent. In the United States, Roosevelt's 'New Deal' was also, in effect, a social democratic response to the great depression. Inspired by and based on John Maynard Keynes' economic analysis, the New Deal stressed the importance of the state regulating the free market, and accepted the legitimate role of the state in providing support for citizens to help them escape destitution.

Social democracy rests upon a contract between capitalism and society which limits inequality and provides a minimum standard of living for all. This is achieved through provision, via a welfare state, of essential goods and services, employment rights, and social and economic protections. Limits on inequality are maintained through taxation and redistribution and through the provision of services by the state in healthcare, education, and social security. In Europe at least, the principle had been established that the state has a vital role to play not only in promoting economic growth, but also in reducing inequality in order to ensure social cohesion and social stability – to guard against the failure of democracy and descent into barbarism.

Human Rights

The taming of capitalism by social democracy was one way that European governments sought to prevent a repeat of the decades of horror they had just experienced. World War Two also provided the catalyst for the development of the final pillar in our modern system of democracy – the legal protection of fundamental human rights.

That a new fundamental principle of national and international law was needed became abundantly clear when Hermann Goering asserted during the Nuremberg Trials that the murder of 6 million Jews 'was our right! We were a sovereign State and that was strictly our business.'[14] In the aftermath of the Holocaust, the protection of the basic rights of every individual, even against the will of the majority, was now seen as an essential duty of government and a duty which had to be enforced by international law. How governments treat their own citizens could no longer be left purely as a matter of domestic concern.

Through the signing of the United Nations Universal Declaration of Human Rights in 1948, the principle of fundamental human rights, enunciated in the Declaration of the Rights of Man and the Citizen, was finally put into practice. The French Revolution enjoyed, at last, its long-delayed victory. The rights established in the Universal Declaration were arrived at through a debate that encompassed the entire global community. In adopting the Declaration, the nations of the world agreed that every person has the right to life, liberty, and security of person; that every person is equal before the law; that everyone is entitled to freedom of conscience, of religion, of expression, and of assembly; and that every person is entitled to the right to work, to food, to shelter, and to education. In adopting the

Declaration, the world's governments agreed that these rights apply to every human being regardless of race, gender, or social class and are not negotiable on the basis of traditional or local cultural or religious practice. Religious or cultural diversity can be only valid if it does not betray our common humanity.

Since the Declaration's signing, a body of international law and an array of institutions have been established around the world to protect the rights of citizens. Three regional human rights systems have been set up. The European human rights system is the most developed, but regional systems are also in place in the Americas and in Africa. Independent Human Rights Commissions have also been established by many governments around the world to protect human rights within national boundaries.

The creation of the International Criminal Court in 2001 marked a further strengthening of the international human rights system. It has been established to act when a state commits serious human rights abuses and is unwilling or unable to prosecute the perpetrators itself. In 2012, the Court issued its first ever verdict, convicting Thomas Lubanga Dyilo of conscripting child soldiers in the Democratic Republic of Congo. Also in 2012, it set legal precedent by sentencing Charles Taylor to 50 years in prison for aiding and abetting rebels who carried out atrocities in Sierra Leone during its harrowing civil war.

Our modern system of democracy can be seen then to be comprised of six pillars, each of which acts as a defense against the abuse of power by pathologically disordered leaders and elites. These are political participation through democratic elections and direct participation of citizens in government, the rule of law applied equally to all, constitutional constraints on the power of government, a prohibition on the imposition of state sponsored ideology, social democracy to ensure social stability, and the protection of fundamental human rights through international law.

The fact that these pillars of democracy do indeed act as constraints on the actions of pathological elites can be seen in the speed with which they dismantle these defenses once they get their hands on power. Stalin's dismantling of democracy in Eastern Europe serves as an illustrative example.

Dismantling Democracy – Stalin in Eastern Europe

Stalin's occupation of Eastern Europe at the end of World War Two provided him with the opportunity to impose his pathological vision upon eight separate European countries. In doing so, as author and journalist Anne Applebaum has meticulously documented,[15] he followed a clear blueprint for tearing down the defenses that each country had built to protect against tyranny.

Eliminating the Rule of Law

Stalin's first step was to install puppet leaders as heads of the interim governments in each country. For this, he chose men who had spent decades in Moscow and had emerged from his purges as true believers, men certain to obey his every command. All immediately began to establish the central instrument of Stalin's power – secret police forces designed to instil terror. Across Eastern Europe, copies of the Soviet NKVD were set up, including Poland's Security Service (Urzad Bezpieczenstwa or SB), Hungary's State Security Agency (Allamvedelmi Osztaly or AVO), East Germany's Ministry for State Security or Stasi as it became known, and the Czechoslovak State Security (Statni Bezpecnost or StB).

As in the USSR, state violence and surveillance were used to subdue the population. The targeting of children was a common tactic. Anne Applebaum tells of the arrest of 15-year-old Gisela Gneist in eastern Germany.[16] Gisela and her friends had formed their own 'political party' to discuss the idea of democracy that they had heard about on American armed forces radio. She was arrested in December 1945, along with two dozen of her teenage friends. Under the stress of torture, Gisela confessed that she had been part of a counter-revolutionary organization. She was found guilty by a military tribunal and imprisoned in the former Nazi concentration camp of Sachsenhausen. Farther south, in Hungary, 16-year-old George Bien suffered a similar fate.[17] He was arrested for owning a short-wave radio, tortured and forced to sign a 30-page Russian confession, of which he didn't understand a single word. Bien was sent to the Gulag camps of Kolyma.

The use of terror quickly came to replace the rule of law across Eastern Europe. Arbitrary arrests, torture as a means of forcing false confessions, convictions without fair trial, and the use of random imprisonment to fulfill the labor needs of the Gulag became the new norms. The most fundamental defense against pathological elites – the rule of law – had been demolished.

Eliminating Electoral Democracy

At the Yalta Conference in February 1945, Stalin had promised Roosevelt and Churchill that free elections would be allowed in the Soviet held nations of Eastern Europe. Stalin, of course, had no intention of honoring this promise. Under his instructions, the region's newly installed puppet leaders set about eliminating electoral democracy and establishing single party states. For the sake of optics, however, mock elections were needed. In Yugoslavia, the Yugoslav People's Front, the only party permitted on the ballot, was declared to have won with 90 percent of the vote. In Bulgaria, where opposition parties called for a boycott in protest at the rigging of the election, the communists seized the opportunity and declared victory. In Poland, Stanislaw Mikolajczyk, well known to the Polish public as former Prime Minister-in-exile in London during the war, tried to hold Stalin to the promise of free elections. Widespread violence, torture, and murder of Mikolajczyk's supporters was Stalin's response.

The communists then falsified the results of the election and installed Stalin's proxy, Bierut, as Polish President. There was, from then on, no authentic political opposition to the Communist Party in Poland for the next 30 years.

In Hungary the communists suffered a very public rebuke when they received only 17 percent of the vote in the election held there in October 1945. Their response was absurd. They claimed that although they had only won some 17 percent of the vote, that 17 percent represented the working class, which deserved a much larger role in government. They then proceeded to take the majority of seats in parliament and the major roles in government, and set out systematically to destroy the opposition. The leader of the main opposition party, Bela Kovacs, was arrested and imprisoned in the Soviet Union. A similar fate awaited anyone who dared oppose the communists' evisceration of democratic politics. Another high-profile victim was Sara Karig, who had been a member of the Hungarian Social Democratic Party during the war and a member of the anti-Nazi resistance.[18] She had helped hundreds of Hungarian Jews escape the Nazis by helping them acquire false papers. In 1947, while serving as chief election officer in Central Budapest, she reported voting fraud to the police. The following day she was arrested, tortured, and sent to the Soviet Gulag camp in Vorkuta. Within a year of her arrest, the Communist Party ruled Hungary alone. The abolition of electoral democracy across the bloc was soon complete.

The Imposition of State Doctrine

Having undermined the rule of law, and dismantled electoral democracy, the communists now turned their attention to imposing the new state religion: Stalinism. For this to happen, actual religion had to be eliminated first. Anti-church propaganda became ever more virulent. In East Germany, Free German Youth gangs appeared at church meetings and heckled those inside.

Public tribunals were held to interrogate children suspected of having religious beliefs, and children were expelled from schools for refusing to renounce their religion. Church schools were nationalized, monasteries closed down and the teaching of religion in schools forbidden. Across the bloc, priests were rounded up in waves of arrests. By 1953, around 1,000 priests were behind bars in Poland alone. The new secret police forces also sought to recruit priests into their ranks to help preach the new state ideology. In 1949 Stalin instructed the eastern bloc governments to '...force priests to spread the ideas of Marx, Engels and Lenin through religious classes and sermons...'

With religion driven underground, the communists now instigated a system aimed at schooling everyone, from kindergarten to the workplace, in the new state ideology. Public displays of violence were used to enforce compliance. In Poland, for example, armed secret policemen raided a secondary school near the town of Sobieszyn and beat the students viciously for not adhering sufficiently to the new Stalinist ideology. Youth groups became particular targets, as the communist authorities viewed them as essential tools for re-educating the next generation. The way in which the communists took control of youth organizations provides a clear example of the process Andrew Lobaczewski described of how a pathological minority takes control of a larger group. Initially the changes were gradual. First someone at the top would be replaced; then he or she would appoint a new deputy; then the deputy would appoint new members and so on. It was clear to members of the organizations what was happening. As one scout leader recalled: 'Each month, new people began gradually infiltrating the scouting movement. There was one, Kosinski, said to be a scout leader. He was as much a scout leader as I am a ballet dancer. He was a [secret police] officer.'[19] Resistance was met by arrest and imprisonment. One teacher targeted by the communists, Alajos Kovacs, recalled that, 'we were shocked, we did not even know why they were attacking us, we could not understand what had happened. Because of this incomprehension, we began to try – in a masochistic, self-defeating way – to understand what had gone wrong, what we had done wrong.'[20] Some of the communists leaders involved in the destruction of youth groups and other civil society movements later recalled how their tactics were consciously based on the 'general law that an organized small group could impose its will on a larger heterogeneous group.'[21] He could equally have said, the general law that a small pathological group could impose its will on a larger group comprised of the psychologically normal majority.

Crushing Human Rights

The replacement of the rule of law by state terror signaled the end of human rights protections across Eastern Europe, as individual freedoms were replaced by constant surveillance by the security police. By 1954, the Polish secret police's 'register of criminal and suspicious elements' had grown to contain 6 million names, or one in three of the adult population. Waves of arrests and investigations were now the norm. Many of those arrested were sent straight to the camps of Stalin's Gulag. Regimes across the bloc also built camps of their own. Between 1949 and 1953, the Czechoslovak regime ran a group of 18 camps near Jachymov where prisoners worked in uranium mines to extract material for the Soviet nuclear weapons program. Death rates in the camps were high. The best-known camps built by the Romanian regime were sited along the route of the Danube-Black Sea canal. At their height, the Romanian Gulag held around 180,000 people.[22] The communist regimes in Bulgaria and Yugoslavia also built labor camps. In Bulgaria these camps continued to exist well into the 1970s, long after the majority of Soviet camps had been closed.

Many people, however, were never allowed the chance of survival that the Gulag camps offered, as the authorities terrorized their populations into compliance. Anne Applebaum again tells the story of one Hungarian peasant whose campfire got out of control and burned his field.[23] No one was harmed and the harvest was not damaged. The secret police, however, labeled this an act of criminal arson and a crime against the state. Amidst a burst of national publicity, the man was convicted, sentenced to death, and executed. His daughter remembered that as they entered the courthouse for the trial, the gallows were already being built outside. Across Eastern Europe, how the state treated its citizens was now firmly, once again, a matter for the state alone to decide.

In her book *Iron Curtain*, Applebaum concludes that the destruction of Eastern European societies by Stalin and the Bolsheviks reveals an unpleasant truth about human nature:

> if enough people are sufficiently determined, and if they are backed by adequate resources and force, then they can destroy ancient and apparently permanent legal, political, educational and religious institutions, sometimes for good. And if civil society could be so deeply damaged in nations as disparate, as historic and as culturally rich as those of Eastern Europe, then it can be similarly damaged anywhere. If nothing else, the history of post-war Stalinization proves just how fragile 'civilisation' can turn out to be.[24]

Democracy as a Moral System

Democracy places limits on those in power. It reduces the scope for recourse to violence. It forbids the abuse of state power against individuals and against sub-sections of society. It reduces inequalities in wealth and power and seeks to provide equality of access to the law and equality of political participation. A democratic society demands that its members limit the pursuit of their self-interest to the extent that the rights of their fellow citizens require it. It requires that citizens treat each other with the respect due them as autonomous individuals with the right to pursue their lives as they see fit. And it requires a commitment to the common good. In return for complying with these demands, democracy produces the public goods that people of all nations have struggled for centuries to achieve, namely peace, justice, freedom, equality, and community.

For many people these demands are difficult to comply with. For people with dangerous personality disorders, they are demands which they are psychologically incapable of submitting to. Moreover, the public goods which democracy produces are experienced by them as the antithesis of the type of society they desire. Psychopaths lack the capacity to react to other people's feelings with feelings of their own, and so have a terrifying ability to treat people without conscience. They view other people as things to be manipulated and exploited rather than as fellow citizens whose rights are to be respected. Their disorder leaves them prone to acts of violence, criminality, and corruption. People with narcissistic personality disorder have minds structured to convince them of their own superiority. They are fixated on adulation, authority, and power. Their disorder is such that they are psychologically incapable of seeing others as equals. Authoritarian, envious, amoral, and contemptuous of others, they are likely to react to anyone who challenges them with aggression. Their sense of entitlement means that they view the exploitation of others as their natural right. People with paranoid personality disorder have minds frozen in a perpetual state of emergency. They can perceive others only as a threat and continually search for vulnerable scapegoats on whom to focus their anxiety. Their constant suspiciousness and distrust of others acts as an acid that dissolves meaningful social relationships. Their combative and suspicious nature often elicits a hostile response in others, leading to conflict and confusion. In situations of civil unrest, they play a central role in fomenting hatred against enemies, real and imagined, and have the energy and passion to organize and mobilize others to participate in acts of mass oppression.

People with these disorders are unable to accept the constraints of living within a democratic society. The language of democracy – fairness, equality, autonomy, freedom of conscience, freedom of thought, freedom for every individual to find meaning in life, the right to dignity, and equality of social relationships – is a language which is utterly incomprehensible to them. People with these disorders struggle to live within democracy's moral strictures and, should the opportunity arise, will gladly tear down the constraints which democracy imposes upon them.

If we are to protect the public goods which democracy provides, we must limit the influence of psychopaths and people with narcissistic and paranoid personality disorders. Unfortunately, however, the conditions which empower people with these disorders are endemic in societies around the world. Levels of global poverty are such that in many countries the rule of law for the majority of citizens is no more than a cruel promise. In the United States and Europe, major political and economic institutions have for decades now fostered a culture of selfish individualism and greed. Religion too has proven itself to be a woefully inadequate guide for individual and collective morality. Selective quotation from the sacred texts of Islam, Christianity, and Judaism continues to cause a spiral of hatred, war, and suffering.

Such context matters not only because it empowers the minority with dangerous personality disorders. It matters because context plays a decisive role in influencing the behavior of the normal majority. As we have seen, human nature, for the majority of human beings, is an extremely malleable thing. For most of us, our beliefs and behaviors vary depending on the circumstances in which we have been brought up and the context within which we live. This basic fact means that, as psychologist Steve Pinker describes it, human nature comprises a mix of both inner demons and better angels. Motives like predation, dominance, competition, and vengeance which impel us to violence and greed, exist alongside motives like compassion, cooperation, fairness, self-control, and reason that, under the right circumstances, impel us toward peace, reciprocity, and other-regarding altruism. If the conditions which favor our better angels prevail, violence and excessive greed are low. If conditions which favor fear, insecurity, and intolerance hold sway, our inner demons win out and violence and greed increase.

This psychological malleability of the majority of humanity, allied with the fixed malevolent nature of the minority with dangerous personality disorders, means that this minority can gain enormous influence over the majority when circumstances allow, not least during periods of instability, societal crises, and uncertainty. Those conditions which constrain the worst aspects of human nature are those which democratic systems seek to achieve: fair and effective application of the rule of law, just and transparent government, an absence of poverty and destitution, a greater tolerance of diversity. There is therefore a crucial link between human behavior and effective democracy. The more progress we make toward truly democratic societies, the more likely we will be to behave with humanity toward one another. The further we move from democracy's ideals, the more intolerant and aggressive we become. Our future depends crucially on us recognizing this basic psychological fact about ourselves and acting upon it.

One psychologist who has stressed the role that democracy plays as a defense against those with psychological disorders is psychoanalyst and leadership expert Manfred Kets de Vries. He writes that benevolent dictatorship is a theoretical possibility but adds:

rule by a solitary leader typically ends in servile obedience to authority and abuse of human rights. In contrast, democracy (though flawed) safeguards human dignity, protects individual freedoms, assures free choice, and gives people a voice in decisions that affect their destiny, allowing them to work for a better future for their children. Humankind's desire for justice and fair play makes democracy possible. Humankind's capacity for injustice makes democracy necessary.'[25]

To save the next generation from the human misery that would accompany the demise of democracy, Kets De Vries urges us to do everything in our power to prevent such a situation from ever again coming to pass.[26]

The system of democracy which has been built over centuries by successive generations can best be seen as a system of institutions and practices, based on fundamental moral principles, which serve to protect societies from a psychologically disordered minority, and from our own worst natures. The history of democracy has been a history of human moral and spiritual development. While equating democracy with morality may sound arrogant or imperialistic to some, from the view point of the victims of history's tyrants, and the many who still suffer under tyranny, it will simply appear as a self-evident fact.

5. Destroying Democracy

Capitalism and Democracy

Neither the dictatorship of theocracy nor that of capital is compatible with the belief in democracy as the underlying principle for organising society.

Richard Swift, The No-Nonsense Guide to Democracy

The twentieth century, which saw the horrors of Stalin, Hitler, Mao, and Pol Pot, was a century characterized by the struggle between capitalism and democracy. From within the fissures created by early capitalism, the tyrants of the twentieth century emerged to murder millions and devastate continents. In the West, the trauma of this experience resulted in a compromise between capitalism and democracy, in which the excesses of capitalism were brought under control through measures to limit inequalities and redistribute wealth in order to maintain social stability. Today that compromise has unraveled and is allowing this century's tyrants to emerge from the extremes in wealth and poverty that contemporary capitalism has created. People with dangerous personality disorders thrive on such extremes, where the norms of fairness, equality, and dignity which characterize democracy, are absent.

Inequality is dangerous because it empowers those with the disorders we are considering, and capitalism today is fueling inequality to a degree not seen for over half a century. To understand the extent to which contemporary capitalism is empowering dangerous individuals we must look at both extremes. We must look at the world's poorest countries where the absence of the safeguards of democracy is resulting in slavery, exploitation, endless war, and violent religious extremism. And we must look at the world's richest countries, and in particular at the United States, where extremes of wealth have undermined both democracy and the social fabric upon which it depends.

To recognize the fact that contemporary capitalism is the root cause of much of the dysfunction in today's world, however, does not mean that we should call for the destruction of capitalism, as was argued a century ago. Capitalism is the only system we know of that can bring people out of poverty. It is the only system we know of through which countries can gain the resources needed to build the institutions of democracy. Because of this reality, capitalism is a crucial tool for reducing the threat that people with dangerous personality disorders pose to societies. But capitalism can only play this supportive role if it is in accord with the values and practices of democracy. When the dominant values of capitalism are in opposition to the values of democracy, as they were in the early twentieth century and are again today, then capitalism becomes an enemy of democracy and the common good, and a friend of dangerously psychologically disordered individuals.

How Poverty Empowers Dangerous Personalities

Africa, the Middle East, and south Asia provide examples of the complex ways in which poverty and the absence of the safeguards of democracy empower psychopaths and leave entire populations at their mercy.

Sub-Saharan Africa is the most impoverished region in the world today, home to 70 percent of the world's 1,000,000,000 poorest people.[1] Chronic poverty coexists alongside a wealth of natural resources including oil, diamonds, and precious minerals. This combination of mineral wealth and endemic poverty has resulted in Africa becoming the most war-torn continent on the planet. In the 1990s, 31 countries, 3 out of 4 nations on the continent, suffered war, ethnically based violence, or genocide.

India, the world's largest democracy, is today host to the worst undernourishment in the world. Around half of all children in India are undernourished, almost twice the level in sub-Saharan Africa. Over 400 million Indian citizens are struggling to survive on around one dollar a day.[2] This endemic poverty leaves millions of poor people vulnerable to violence and exploitation. Over 27 million people worldwide are victims of forced labor and sexual exploitation.[3] India today is home to more slaves than any other country in the world.

Across the Middle East, poverty and the absence of democracy have resulted in decades of war, the persistence of kleptocratic governments intent on enriching themselves rather than developing their societies, and the emergence of support for religious extremism.

In each of these cases, extreme poverty provides the most ruthless in society with opportunities to further their interests – through war, exploitation, and oppression – at enormous costs to the people in each region.

Africa's Wars

We had all been in the rain together until yesterday. Then a handful of us – the smart, and the lucky and hardly ever the best – had scrambled for the one shelter our former rulers left, and had taken it over and barricaded themselves in.
Chinua Achebe

New York Times journalist Jeffrey Gettleman has an explanation for Africa's decades of almost constant war. 'There is a very simple reason why some of Africa's bloodiest, most brutal wars never seem to end,' he writes. 'They are not really wars, at least not in the conventional sense.' Africa's wars today, Gettleman argues, are not struggles against colonialism, tyranny, or apartheid – they are wars motivated and financed by crime. The combatants have neither an ideology nor a set of clear goals that, once achieved, would result in the end of the conflict. Instead,

Africa's wars are mainly the result of rebel leaders carving out fiefdoms for themselves in order to exploit the continent's gold, diamonds, copper, tin, and other valuable minerals. 'If you'd like to call this war, fine,' Gettleman writes, 'but what is spreading across Africa like a viral pandemic is actually just opportunistic, heavily armed banditry...Most of today's African fighters are not rebels with a cause; they're predators.'

This predation that Gettleman warns about has been clearly evident in the largest war in Africa's history – the war in the Democratic Republic of Congo. The DR Congo is one of the poorest countries in the world, but also one richly endowed with natural wealth. The conflict that has ravaged the country since 1996 has cost the lives of over 5 million people, around 3 million of whom have been children. The war began as direct result of the 1994 Rwandan genocide. In the spring and early summer of that year, an estimated 800,000 men, women, and children were systematically murdered in Rwanda – almost three-quarters of the country's Tutsi population. The massacres continued for 100 days before being halted by the Tutsi rebels of the Rwandan Patriotic Front (RPF). As the genocide ended, a mass exodus took place as Hutus fled to neighboring countries, including DR Congo. Among those fleeing were the Forces Armees Rwandaises (FAR), who had been responsible for the genocide. The FAR used the refugee camps in DR Congo, where millions of Hutu refugees had gathered, as bases to regroup and launch attacks back into Rwanda. The persistence of these attacks eventually resulted in the invasion of the DRC by the Rwandan RPF, under its leader Paul Kagame.

The initial phase of the Congo war was short lived because the armed forces of the DRC, under its dictator Mobutu Sese Seko, were deeply corrupt and chaotic. Having seized power at independence in 1960, Mobuto had set about plundering his country's vast natural wealth, rather than seeking to develop the nation. By the early 1980s he was one of the world's wealthiest men, with a fortune estimated at around $5,000,000,000. His lavish portfolio of properties included a palace modeled on Versailles in Paris and a replica of the Imperial Palace in Beijing.[4] Despite his vast personal wealth, Mobutu's soldiers were seldom paid. Instead Mobutu encouraged them to steal from the DR Congo's population as a means to make a living: 'You have guns; you don't need a salary,' he told them. At senior levels in the army, corruption and self-enrichment were the norm. Mobutu's generals sold the air force's last fighter jets and transport aircraft to arms dealers and pocketed the proceeds, while senior commanders in the east of the country sold vital military intelligence to the Rwandan army ahead of the RPF's invasion. As a result, Kigame's forces faced little opposition as they marched toward Kinshasa, forcing Mobutu to flee the country.

Laurent Kabila, who Kigame installed as a figurehead president, presided over the DR Congo for only 15 months before the war began again. When Kabila began to recruit Rwandan Hutu, many of whom had been responsible for the Rwandan genocide, into the Congolese army, Rwanda responded by launching a second invasion. This time the coalition of countries that Rwanda had assembled to oust Mobutu split down the middle, making this a truly pan-African war. The looting of Congo's vast natural resources now assumed a major role in the conflict.[5] When Laurent Kabila was assassinated in 2001, he was succeeded by his son Joseph Kabila, who quickly negotiated an end to the fighting. After 5 years of war, and millions of deaths, the second phase of the Congo war ended. A third phase, however, continues in 2017, as rival militias in eastern Congo continue to terrorize the local population in battles to control the region's mineral resources. While many of those controlling the fighting have grown rich, the Democratic Republic of Congo is poorer today than it was half a century ago.

In his account of the war in DR Congo, Jason Stearns

compares the political system in Congo with a centrifuge in which the most ruthless remain at the center, while those with any conscience are flung to the fringes of political life.[6] The same is true across much of Africa. Across the continent, weak or failed states produce political systems that reward ruthlessness and marginalize anyone whose vision extends beyond power and self-enrichment. Disordered personalities thrive under these conditions. A few examples will illustrate the point. In Liberia and Sierra Leone, in a tactic which mirrored that of the Khmer Rouge, warlord Charles Taylor's recruitment of teenagers as soldiers led to that civil war becoming known as the 'children's war'. Officers praised their child soldiers' lack of inhibition and their ability to rape and kill without compunction. Up to half of all rebel militia in Sierra Leone were between 8 and 14 years old. Numbed by cocaine, children systematically terrorized the country, hacking off the hands or feet of unarmed civilians. In Sudan, Omar al-Bashir seized power in 1989 with a copy of the Koran in one hand and a rifle in the other. He vowed that, 'Anyone who betrays the nation does not deserve the honor of living.' Al-Bashir introduced a form of Islamic law that allowed for crucifixion, death by stoning, and death for renouncing Islam. Under his rule up to 2 million Sudanese have been denied 'the honor of living' as a result of war, famine, and disease. The war has resulted in the division of the country into Sudan and South Sudan, but the violence has not ceased. Angola is another example. There a 27-year-long civil war impoverished another African nation rich in natural resources. More than 350,000 people died in the civil war while both sides profited massively from the fighting. Rebel leader Jonas Savimbi amassed well over $2,000,000,000 from the diamond mines under his control. The government of Eduardo dos Santos benefited equally by looting Angola's oil wealth, estimated to be equal to the total aid for the entire continent. When the civil war ended in 2002, the 60 richest people in Angola had a combined wealth in excess of

$4,000,000,000. Ninety-five percent of Angola's 16 million people live on less than a dollar a day. One quarter of the nation's children die before the age of five.

Psychopaths as Predators on the Poor

Democracy is not just the right to vote, it is the right to live in dignity.
Naomi Klein

As the world's largest democracy, India is a symbol to the world. Its 1951 Adult Suffrage Act, which granted the right to vote to all Indian citizens regardless of gender or religion, was the largest single act of freedom in all of human history. At a stroke, 350 million people became participants in their own future, with the right to decide how they would be governed. India's democratic progress at that historic moment stands in stark contrast with its giant neighbor, where just 2 years earlier Mao Zedong proclaimed the establishment of the People's Republic of China, doubling the number of people worldwide living under the tyranny of communism. The heritage of India's freedom movement and its founding leaders, particularly Mahatma Gandhi, provide ideals that continue to inspire India and the world. India's democracy is remarkable too because of India's diversity of religions, languages, and ethnicities. Thanks to its secular constitution, India can boast of having had a Muslim President, a Sikh Prime Minister, and a Christian head of the ruling party, all sharing in the same governing coalition.[7] Despite these remarkable successes, endemic poverty continues to undermine India's ability to deliver fully on the promise of democracy, and in particular to protect its poorest citizens from exploitation by those with dangerous personality disorders. This is most evident in the extent to which India's poor are subjected to slavery and enforced prostitution. India today has at least 18 million modern slaves, which is over five times more than any other country in the world. The main reason for this is poverty. In India, and across the developing world, poverty translates into a lack of resources for the enforcement of law and order. Washington DC spends about $850 per person, per year on policing. India spends less than 13 cents per person. Across most of sub-Saharan Africa the figure is lower still. In their book *The Locust Effect*, Gary Haugen and Victor Boutros provide a disturbing catalogue of violence and oppression inflicted upon the world's poor which occurs chiefly because the rule of law is absent. 'Violence,' they write, 'is as much a part of what it means to be poor as being hungry, sick, homeless, or jobless...violence is frequently the problem that poor people are most concerned about. It is one of the core reasons they are poor in the first place, and one of the primary reasons they stay poor.'[8] In the relative safety of the developed world, the authors continue, it is easy to, 'forget that the human population in your city is actually capable of tremendous predatory violence in the absence of a coercive system of law and order.' In the developed world, 'the presence of massive and expensive law enforcement systems help us to forget about the germ of violence that is always in the air.'

Haugen and Boutros tell the story of Mariamma, who was held for years in slavery in a brick factory in India. Mariamma's enslavement began when the brick factory's owner approached her and her colleagues and offered them $40 each to cover the costs of moving to their new jobs at his factory. Once they arrived they were beaten by local thugs and told that they could not leave until they had repaid their 'debt'. Their paltry pay was such that they had no prospect of ever being able to do so. During their imprisonment, the women and girls were repeatedly raped by the owner and his son. When Mariamma and her colleagues finally managed to escape and flee to the police, the police sided with the wealthy factory owner. It took six-and-a-half years before a trial was heard, and at that trial the judge acquitted the owner and his son of all charges without listening to witnesses or considering any evidence. In the whole of India, where millions are held in forced labor, Haugen and Boutros could only identify five perpetrators who have done substantial prison time for enslavement over the last 15 years.[9]

The story of Meena Hasina, recounted in Nicholas Kristof and Sheryl Wudunn's book *Half the Sky*,[10] illustrates how India's poor also suffer extensively at the hands of sexual predators. Meena was born in the northern Indian state of Bihar. Before she was 10 years old she was kidnapped and sold to a brothel owner. When she was 12, she was taken to the brothel where she was beaten, 'with a belt, with sticks, with iron rods...They showed me swords and said they would kill me if I didn't agree. Four or five times, they brought customers in, and I still resisted, and they kept beating me. Finally, they drugged me...' When Meena was unconscious, the brothel owners raped her. Beaten and raped into submission, Meena began a life of prostitution in which she was forced to have sex with ten or more customers a day. The brothel owners used terror to keep the girls they held captive from running away. Any girl not obeying instructions was tied and beaten savagely, while all the other girls were forced to watch. Local police officers, instead of acting to protect the girls, were frequent clients at the brothel.

The absence of the rule of law, effective law enforcement, and mechanisms for police accountability mean that India's poor also suffer daily from police predation. For many poor people in India, and across the developing world, the police are just another criminal gang. In the absence of Habeas Corpus, people can be arrested and left to languish in prison without charge for years in pre-trial detention. Around 30 million people are currently awaiting trial in India, with an average wait of 15 years before their case comes to court. In most cases, the time an individual spends in prison awaiting trial exceeds the maximum sentence that could be imposed if he or she were to be found guilty. Such a system provides the police with a golden opportunity to arrest innocent people and demand bribes for their release. Refusal to pay can mean years in prison awaiting trial.

In poor countries, widespread corruption means that many judges too have their price. Those charged with serious crimes and wealthy enough to buy their way out almost always walk free. Radha Vinod Raju, the former Director General of the National Investigation Agency in India, has warned that due to the vanishingly low conviction rates for wealthy defendants, the deterrent effect of India's criminal justice system for wealthy and well-connected criminals is close to vanishing point.[11]

Across the developing world, the fundamental systems of law and order have been so useless for so long that violent criminals know they can prey on the most vulnerable with no prospect of being caught. Such lawlessness is a dream come true for the world's psychopaths, bullies, and thieves. It is a daily nightmare for the majority of the world's poorest and most vulnerable people.

Religious Extremism

Men never do evil so completely and cheerfully as when they do it from religious conviction.
Blaise Pascal

Every country that harbors an extremist Islamic insurgency today contains a poverty-stricken population suffering under a corrupt government. Support for violent Islamic groups such as al-Qaeda, the Taliban in Afghanistan, Islamic State in Iraq and Syria, and Boko Haram in Nigeria, can be explained, at least in part, as a violent response to elites who continue to enrich themselves at the expense of their impoverished populations.

Ayman al-Zawahiri, who succeeded Osama Bin Laden as head of al-Qaeda, cited as the root cause of injustice across the Middle East, north Africa, and west Asia, 'regimes that are corrupt, rotten and allied with the Crusaders...these corrupt and rotten regimes are the reason behind economic injustice and corruption, the political oppression, and social detachment.' The evidence supports his assertion. Take Afghanistan, for example. Top of the list of reasons cited by prisoners in Afghanistan for joining the Taliban was not the call of Islam or occupation by US forces, but the corruption of the Afghan government. Transparency International consistently places Afghanistan among the three or four most corrupt countries in the world. According to anti-corruption activist Sarah Chayes, the Afghan government is best viewed, 'not as a government at all but as a vertically integrated criminal organisation.'[12] Endemic corruption means that Afghans more often suffer at the hands of the law than receive the protection of it. The annual sum of daily shakedowns people suffer at the hands of the country's police, doctors, judges, or government clerks is estimated to be around $4,000,000,000.[13]

Nigeria is another example. Here government corruption and endemic police brutality fuel support for the extreme violence of Boko Haram. State governors and politicians embezzled around $250,000,000,000 between 2005 and 2007.[14] According to Human Rights Watch, 'the Nigeria Police Force has become a symbol in Nigeria of unfettered corruption, mismanagement, and abuse', and are viewed by the population, 'more as predators than protectors'. The Nigerian police routinely round up random citizens in public places, including mass arrests at restaurants, markets, and bus stops. Those arrested are taken at gunpoint to police stations where the police demand money in return for their release. Failure to pay can result in sexual assault, torture, or even death in police custody.

This pattern of corrupt governments enriching themselves at the expense of their populations, allied with everyday police predation, was the backdrop for the uprisings of the 2011 Arab

Spring. Every country that experienced mass protests during the Arab Spring was a kleptocracy in which ruling families amassed enormous wealth while economies faltered. In every country, state oppression in the form of arbitrary arrest and torture was used widely to suppress dissent. The overthrow of such long-standing kleptocrats was the primary aim of the millions of protestors who took to the streets during the uprisings across the region. The uprisings had a promising start. Within months, four of the region's most entrenched dictators – Zine El Abidine Ben-Ali in Tunisia, Hosni Mubarak in Egypt, Muammar Gaddafi in Libya, and Ali Abdullah Saleh in Yemen – had been forced from power. These successes, however, were short lived. In Bahrain widespread peaceful protests were suppressed by the authorities with the help of Saudi Arabia. In Syria a bloody civil war erupted in response to Bashar al-Assad's crackdown on peaceful protesters there. Libya too descended into war following the overthrow of Gaddafi. And in Egypt, the regime of Hosni Mubarak has been replaced by an equally repressive military dictatorship under Abdel Fattah el-Sisi. The Arab Spring uprisings had been preceded 2 years earlier by the violent suppression of the pro-democracy demonstrations of the Green Revolution in Iran.

The failure of the Arab Spring in most countries in the region has crushed the hopes of millions. Faced with the immovable burdens of corrupt kleptocratic leaders and endemic police predation, many people across the region have come to believe that change can only be brought about through the violent overthrow of the existing regimes and their replacement with strict Islamic law. After decades of war, suffering, and oppression, the imposition of justice and order, promised by the region's Islamic insurgents, is drawing many fighters and sympathizers to their cause.

While religious fundamentalism may appear to offer a radical alternative to corruption and state violence, in practice, however, it provides ample opportunities for those with dangerous personality disorders to thrive. The connection between religion and violence, of which al-Qaeda and ISIS are just the most recent manifestations, has of course a very long history. It is a history that is not confined to Islam, and the link between religion and violence is not coincidental. On the contrary, a number of characteristics of many religions serve to attract violent individuals and propel them to positions of influence and power. Recall again the role of ideology in enabling pathological elites to seize power. A compelling ideology can mobilize mass support; it helps to disguise the pathological group's true nature and intent; and it can serve to justify acts of mass violence conducted by the pathological group in its efforts to right injustice. The more strongly the ideology resonates with the values and concerns of the psychologically normal majority, the greater its value in helping pathological groups rise to power. Religious ideologies are among the most powerful ideologies there are. Unfortunately, a number of the core characteristics of many religions also resonate with people with personality disorders. These characteristics include the claim to absolute truth, an insistence that proof is not necessary, widespread use of censorship to suppress dissent, and divine license to kill those who disagree. Taken together these claims form the perfect recipe for tyrannical rule. It is a recipe which combines the unwavering certainty of the narcissist, the ruthless inhumanity of the psychopath, and the paranoia of those who claim to be attuned to the mysterious workings of evil in this world. In the words of author Reza Aslan, religious ideology transforms those who should be considered murderers and thugs into soldiers sanctioned by God.

If the twentieth century was the bloodiest period of political experimentation the world has ever witnessed, then ISIS is simply a continuation of that dynamic into the present century. An extended period of brutal war has traumatized many societies across the Middle East, creating the conditions for a deeply psychopathic organization to gain power with a measure of public support. Their ideology promises a utopian future, as Eric Hoffer described, but between the present unjust reality and the realization of the utopian vision lie enemies who must be destroyed. The present injustices and the lure of a perfect future are sufficient to sway not only fanatics but many ordinary people to their cause. As is the case in Africa's wars, the sectarian wars raging across the Middle East, west Asia, and north Africa today are acting as a centrifuge in which only the most ruthless can remain at the center, while those with any conscience are flung to the fringes. The opposing forces of pathological elites clinging corruptly to power, and pathological extremists waging war under the banner of religious fundamentalism, are causing that centrifuge to spin ever more out of control, with devastating consequences for the millions of poor and powerless people trapped in between.

Capitalism as Cause and Solution of Poverty and Violence

Extreme poverty is one of the major issues fueling Africa's wars, India's slavery and sexual exploitation, and the violent Islamic extremism that blights the Middle East and further afield. Poverty enables dangerous personalities and disempowers the many victims of their violence and exploitation.

Such poverty is the result of a failure of contemporary capitalism. The name that economists give to that failure is the Great Divergence. The Great Divergence refers to the gap in wealth between rich developed nations and the countries of the developing world. But there is another story; that of capitalism's success. The name that economists give to that success is the Great Escape.

Author and financial journalist Martin Wolf points to the two basic economic facts that help explain both the Great

Divergence and the Great Escape. The first fact is that over the last 2 centuries capitalism has created unprecedented levels of economic growth. The result has been, as Nobel Prize winning economist Angus Deaton describes, humanity's 'Great Escape' from disease and deprivation.[15] Until roughly 2 centuries ago, modern economic growth simply didn't happen anywhere in the world. During the 2,000 years separating ancient Greece from pre-Industrial Revolution Europe, living standards around the world barely changed and mere survival was the overriding concern for the vast majority of the world's population. Since the Industrial Revolution began, however, living standards in the world's most developed countries have increased by a factor of several thousand.[16] Between 1820 and 1992, the average income of all the inhabitants of the world increased between 7 and 8 times and the fraction of the world's population in extreme poverty fell from 84 percent to 24 percent.[17]

The person who best understood what has been causing this incredible increase in wealth was Austrian economist Joseph Schumpeter. Schumpeter showed that industrial capitalism, driven by technological advances, is the driving force behind economic growth. Industrial capitalism, Schumpeter realized, relies on the invention of major new technologies, such as the steam engine, the automobile, and the computer. Each new technology allows entrepreneurs, using the financial backing of those with sufficient capital, to create entirely new industries which create millions of jobs and push up living standards. The automotive industry, the oil and gas industries, the aviation industry, the pharmaceuticals industry, the chemicals industry, the computing and communications industries, the defense industry – these are among the major industries that grew out of the invention of new technologies and have made the rich countries rich.

Schumpeter also showed, however, that economic growth is not a smooth process but instead lunges forward through vast, uneven surges. These waves of creative destruction, as Schumpeter called them, rise as each new technology creates a frenzy of economic activity and then peter out as the economic impact of that technology recedes. For Schumpeter, continual disruption is therefore not coincidental to capitalism; it is the mechanism through which economic development occurs. While he fully acknowledged the destructive aspects of creative destruction, Schumpeter argued strenuously that, despite these disruptions, industrial capitalism has benefited humanity enormously. As we have seen, industrial capitalism also generated the colossal social conflicts which shaped the twentieth century. These conflicts – particularly the conflict between capitalism and communism – centered largely on the uneven distribution of the wealth that industrial capitalism created. Despite these conflicts, however, for the first 2 centuries of its history there is no doubt that capitalism has generated wealth for those countries with the know-how to invent new technologies and to benefit from them.

Schumpeter's model of industrial capitalism explains the first of Martin Wolf's basic economic facts: the unprecedented economic dynamism of the last 2 centuries which has fueled the Great Escape from poverty for most of humanity. However, Schumpeter's rosy picture of economic growth is only half of the story. The other half is Martin Wolf's second basic economic fact: the Great Divergence. This has arisen because economic growth rates have varied markedly between countries since the Industrial Revolution. The vast gap in wealth we see between nations today has resulted from the inability of some countries to generate and maintain economic growth over sustained periods. Economists disagree on the reasons that some countries fail to generate growth, but factors such as geographical isolation, poor governance, war, and lack of natural resources all play a major role. The result is today's world, described by Peruvian author Oswaldo de Rivera as one in which a small archipelago of wealthy nations is surrounded and outnumbered by a majority of poor or extremely poor countries. Of the 135 poorest countries in the world today, the majority still have close to 50 percent of their population living in extreme poverty.[18]

The Great Escape, for most of humanity, alongside continuing extreme deprivation for many people as a result of the Great Divergence, are both the fruits of over 2 centuries of industrial capitalism – its success as well as its failure. But in recent decades even industrial capitalism's failure has begun to be addressed. Since 1980, more than 1,000,000,000 people have escaped poverty due to economic growth in China and India alone, as each country has become integrated into the global industrial economy. This is the fastest reduction in poverty in human history. The sharpest decline has occurred in China, where 660 million people have risen out of extreme poverty. The fraction of the population living in poverty in China has fallen from 84 percent to 12 percent. In India, almost 50 million people have escaped extreme poverty as the poverty rate has dropped to 33 percent, down from 60 percent 3 decades ago.

The remarkable successes of India and China demonstrate that industrial capitalism continues to provide an escape route from poverty. Reductions in poverty also mean reductions in violence, as countries gain the resources to build the institutions of law and order, democracy, and human rights needed to restrain their most ruthless and violent citizens. Although progress toward democracy is not inevitable as poverty declines, increases in wealth at least allow for that possibility. The historical experiences of the countries of the rich developed world, and the more recent experiences of China and India, provide a strong argument that continued economic growth, and the more equitable sharing of that growth, is vital if the Great Escape from poverty, disease – and violence – is to spread to those living in the rest of the developing world.

How Inequality is Empowering Dangerous Personalities

The movement against war is sound. I pray for its success. But I cannot help the gnawing fear that the movement will fail if it does not touch the root of all evil – human greed.
Gandhi

In recent times, industrial capitalism has at last started to spread its benefits beyond a few select countries. However, just as industrial capitalism has begun to reduce inequality between nations, a new model of capitalism – financial capitalism – has grown to dominate the global economy. This new model of financial capitalism is marked by massive growth in the banking and financial sectors and differs radically from Schumpeter's industrial capitalism. Unlike industrial capitalism, financial capitalism is not based on the invention of new technologies. It is based entirely on gaining returns from the investment of money. It is a form of capitalism primarily designed to benefit the rich and its effects to date have been disastrous. It has resulted directly in the worst global economic crisis since the 1930s, and has contributed to vast increases in inequality, giving rise to the small class of global super-rich, popularly referred to as the 1 percent. The extreme concentration of wealth that financial capitalism has produced is undermining democracy and social cohesion across the developed world and is providing ample opportunities for those with dangerous personalities to thrive.

The rise of global mega-corporations has contributed crucially to the development of financial capitalism. Over the last 40 years, due to advances in transport and communications technology, including container shipping, air travel, and satellite communication, it became possible for firms to distribute their operations across the world. Within just 30 years, beginning

149

in the 1970s, the number of such multinational corporations multiplied from 7,000 to almost 38,000.[19] At the same time, the size of these firms also increased enormously. One key factor was the repeal of anti-monopoly laws in the United States, which had been in place to limit the size of corporations since the nineteenth century. The repeal of these laws opened the way for a frenzy of mergers and acquisitions and the creation of today's giant global firms.

In 1980 the US banking industry was made up of around 14,000 banks, ranging from small community banks to major global financial corporations. By 2007 most of these institutions were gone and more than 80 percent of the US financial industry's total assets were controlled by only 20 giant companies.[20] The repeal of the Glass-Steagall Act in the United States in 1999 then allowed these new megabanks to operate across both commercial and investment banking. The Glass-Steagall Act, which had been in place for around 60 years, had acted as a safeguard in the financial sector by strictly separating commercial and investment banking, and requiring banks to hold specific levels of cash reserves against their loan liabilities. Now, just as the financial stakes were rocketing, these safeguards were removed.

The rise of a relatively few giant financial institutions concentrated wealth and power into the hands of a small number of corporate leaders and altered the balance of power between governments and financial corporations. This inordinate influence enabled corporations to persuade politicians to rewrite the rules of the global financial system to enable these institutions to maximize their profits by conducting financial transactions on a global scale. Up until the 1990s most governments retained control over the financial transactions that took place across their borders. Many, for example, placed restrictions on the ability of their citizens to take money out of the country or to purchase financial assets abroad. Strict rules were also in place limiting the ability of domestic banks and firms to borrow money from abroad. Short-term lending and borrowing were tightly controlled because they were recognized as having the potential to create serious financial instability.[21] However from the 1990s onwards the deregulation of international financial flows became a key objective of the governments of the United States and the United Kingdom and the accepted policy position of the International Monetary Fund and the World Bank. The free movement of capital across borders which they introduced, along with the widespread adoption of computer technology, enabled financial trading to take place across the world on a scale, and on timescales, never before possible. Unlike the free movement granted to capital, however, fewer mobility rights were granted to people.

Within a decade the global financial economy mushroomed to far outweigh the total value of the real global economy. By 2007, the daily volume of foreign currency transactions had risen to over €3,000,000,000,000, almost 100 times larger than the daily volume of trade.[22] Computer technology and deregulation also enabled the development of complex financial products, particularly credit derivatives, which were a major contributor to the 2008 financial collapse. Between 1997 and 2007 the global market for derivatives rose from $41,000,000,000,000 to $677,000,000,000,000.[23] That is more than 10 times the gross national product of all the countries in the world combined.[24] The sheer scale of money involved allowed corporations to award their executives salaries and bonuses that enabled many individuals in the financial sector to amass considerable wealth. These super-salaries then spread to other non-financial corporations, contributing to an explosion in inequality of incomes and the growth of a tiny elite, the 1 percent, to whom most of the fruits of the economic growth generated by financial capitalism have accrued. Today, Schumpeter's model of industrial capitalism has been eclipsed by a model of financial capitalism which places speculation – not manufacturing – at the core of the global capitalist system. Far from simply oiling the wheels of industry and commerce, the financial sector has grown to dwarf the 'real economy' upon which capitalism had previously relied.

This fundamental change in the nature of capitalism has been facilitated by the ideology of neoliberalism, the dominant economic orthodoxy of our financial age. Neoliberalism is as much a political as an economic ideology, as is evidenced by its major claims. Political scientist Manfred Steger has outlined what these are:[25]

It presents all governments – including democratic governments – as a threat to individual liberty.

Neoliberalism arose just as the communist regimes in the Soviet Union and Eastern Europe were crumbling. This historical context was seized on by neoliberals to present all governments, including democratically elected governments, as a threat to personal freedom.[26]

It promises that the triumph of free markets over governments would strengthen both the economy and individual freedom.

As the magazine *Businessweek* explained to its readers, 'Globalization is about the triumph of markets over governments.'[27] The replacement of the power of governments by the power of the market, neoliberals claim, is the means both to boost economic growth and increase individual freedoms.

It insists that the triumph of markets is inevitable and that there is no alternative.

Neoliberals presented the fall of the Soviet Union as the 'end of history'. The victory of their version of free-market capitalism over every other type of economy, neoliberals assert, is an historic inevitability. There is, they say, no alternative.

It claims that economies work best when governments don't intervene.

A core dogma of neoliberalism is that a market economy, if

left undisturbed by government regulation, will find its own perfectly efficient equilibrium. This powerful image implies that no one is imposing their agenda on others. Rather than being a systematic program by governments and businesses to actively rewrite the rules to benefit themselves, a free market economy is presented as being governed by impersonal forces, akin to the laws of physics.

It claims that the alchemy of neoliberalism will transform greed into gold for all.

Neoliberalism promises to spread wealth, democracy, and freedom across the world, and it promises to do so by basing the entire enterprise on what neoliberals consider to be the essence of human nature – greed. Market forces alone, its proponents claim, will transform the basest human instincts – narcissism, greed, and the ruthless pursuit of wealth and power – into greater wealth and freedom for all.

Like all powerful ideologies, neoliberalism is based on partial truths. It resonates with ordinary people because it promises prosperity and freedom. It resonates with working people's dreams of becoming rich and escaping economic hardship. It also resonates powerfully, however, with those with dangerous personality disorders for whom greed and exploitation are at the core of their nature. By insisting on the subordination of governments to private interests, neoliberals have succeeded in undermining some of the key defenses which Western societies have built over the last 2 centuries to protect citizens from exploitation. By rewriting laws and weakening regulation for decades up to the Financial Crash of 2008, a global financial system has been constructed that enables elites to pursue their own short-term interests, regardless of the consequences of their actions.

The rules governing financial institutions mirror those of the wider economy that neoliberals seek to establish. Author Yves

Smith has summarized the environment within the financial sector as one characterized by weak or absent regulation; where huge incentives fuel a highly aggressive competition for promotion; and where hiring and pay practices incentivize short-term focus, rule-bending, and aggression.[28] In his book *Swimming with Sharks*[29], based on hundreds of interviews with insiders working in the City of London, Joris Luyendijk identifies multiple structural defects within financial institutions which permit, and even encourage, narcissistic and psychopathic behavior. These include enormous conflicts of interest within institutions (which deal in commercial banking and mortgage lending on the one hand and investment banking on the other); the absence of effective independent checks and balances (since ratings agencies and accounting firms are not truly independent and regulators have proven themselves unable to hold banks to account); intense pressure to continually increase profits imposed by shareholders (who look at returns and returns only); the fact that caveat emptor or 'buyer beware' is the accepted legal principle governing the sale of financial products (which means that those who buy complex financial products have no recourse even when those products are aggressively marketed by banks in the knowledge their clients will lose); zero job security (so that individuals are in no position to question practices within the bank and have enormous incentives to comply); a scale and complexity that effectively means that no one is in control (or as former Labor chancellor Alistair Darling remarked, while we often hear of banks that are 'too big to fail', in reality financial institutions today are 'too big to know what's going on'); and, finally, a system in which no one is held responsible. Historically within banking, partners were personally responsible for their organizations. As this is no longer the case, those who take the risks within financial institutions, at all levels including senior management, are not the same people who bear them. In fact, as the Financial Crash demonstrated, the people who actually bear the risks are us.

With opportunities for personal enrichment so high, regulation so lax, and the personal consequences of an individual's actions so low, the culture which has evolved within many financial institutions is characterized by an alarming absence of morality. Many employees have attested to this toxic amoral culture. Former Morgan Stanley employee Frank Portnoy relates how the aggressive environment he worked in made him 'crave the sensation of ripping someone's face off.'[30] He recounts one colleague as saying, 'You have to be a criminal to be good at this business.'[31] Former Goldman Sachs director Nomi Prins admitted, 'To retain supremacy, banks had to prey upon their existing and emerging corporate clients...'[32] Former CEO of Morgan Stanley John Mack was known for his mantra, 'There's blood in the water, let's go kill someone.'[33] And Dick Fuld, the former CEO of Lehman Brothers, told Lehman staff that he wanted to 'rip out their [his competitors] hearts and eat them before they died.' An employee of derivatives trading firm Bankers Trust was caught on tape saying that the firm's objective was 'to lure people into the calm and then just totally fuck 'em.'[34] Other employees tell of an environment where having emotions or being ill are seen as signs of weakness. 'You have to assume this persona without emotions,' one banker recounted. 'I found myself crying in the loo so many times. That's the only place where you can be a human being: in the loo.'[35]

It is to be expected that the absence of basic ethical values on the part of many financial institutions would mean that people with psychopathic and narcissistic personality disorders would find them attractive and rewarding places to work. Psychopaths and narcissists exhibit tremendous energy and push extremely hard to get what they want. They are profoundly competitive and are adept at self-promotion. Financial institutions have found these confident, assertive personalities extremely attractive. One study of 200 high-potential executives found that

3.5 percent fitted the profile of the psychopath.³⁶ This is three-and-a-half times higher than in the general population. All of the individuals identified in the study had traits of the manipulative psychopath: grandiose, deceitful, irresponsible, lacking remorse, and devoid of empathy. In the centrifuge created by the amoral pursuit of personal wealth, it is to be expected that the most ruthless will gravitate toward the center. Thanks to the work of pioneering psychologists such as Alan Goldman, the presence of people with dangerous personality disorders in leadership positions in organizations, and the damage they cause, is no longer an untestable hypothesis. Goldman has shown that it is possible for psychologically trained professionals to use the diagnostic criteria for dangerous personality disorders in the DSM Diagnostic and Statistical Manual of Mental Disorders, with the active cooperation of the individual and organization involved, to link organizational dysfunction to a seriously flawed leader harboring a long-standing personality disorder.³⁷

When the US housing boom began to stall, the financial system began to unravel. The aggressive policies that had been associated with sub-prime lending led to massive levels of mortgage default. This resulted in the downgrading of many of the new derivative products previously deemed as super safe by the ratings agencies. The subsequent drop in the value of derivatives assets far exceeded the slim financial cushions that the banks had maintained, leaving many of them bankrupt. In October 2008 the then Head of the IMF, Dominique Strauss-Kahn, said, 'Intensifying solvency concerns about a number of the largest US-based and European financial institutions have pushed the global financial system to the brink of financial meltdown.'³⁸ Western bankers, with the active assistance of politicians, had bankrupted much of the Western financial system and left little option for governments but to bail them out. This lead to misery for millions who lost their jobs, faced reductions in incomes, or were left with debts that they could not hope to repay. After the crash, as unemployment and home repossessions spiraled upwards, the men at the helm of the major financial institutions responsible for the crisis, however, pocketed fortunes and walked away. To quote just a few examples, the top five executives at Lehman Brothers made over $1,000,000,000 between 2000 and 2007. When their firm went bankrupt, they kept the money. The CEO of Merrill Lynch, Stan O'Neill, received $90 million in 2007 and 2008 and was allowed to resign, after leaving his firm in ruins, with $161 million in severance.[39] In the UK, Fred Goodwin, former Royal Bank of Scotland CEO, was given a £693,000 annual pension after leading the bank to a record £24,000,000,000 loss which necessitated a government bailout.[40] Goodwin later bowed to public anger and agreed to reduce his pension to £342,500 a year. However, he kept a £2.8 million lump sum, on which RBS paid the tax, and a £2.6 million bonus he had been paid in his last year at the company.

The Crisis has changed little. Following bailouts costing billions of taxpayers' money, the largest financial firms are larger than ever. There is little evidence that the predator culture in the financial industry has altered. In 2010 New York Judge Jack B. Weinstein declared during a trial involving financial fraud that the evidence presented, 'laid bare the pernicious and pervasive culture of corruption in the financial services industry... Supervision is seriously negligent; greed and short-term gain are so enormous that fraud and arrogant disregard of others' rights and of ethics almost encourage criminal activities...'[41] In 2012 Goldman Sachs executive director Greg Smith resigned publicly in a letter to the *New York Times* stating that the environment in the firm was as toxic and as destructive as he had ever seen it. He described a culture in which management encouraged employees to rip off the firm's clients, who they regularly referred to as 'muppets'. 'Today, if you make enough money for the firm (and are not currently an axe murderer),' Smith wrote, 'you will be promoted into a position of influence.'[42] In his 2016 book *Other People's Money*, Financial Times journalist John Kay wrote that 'parts of the financial sector today...demonstrate the lowest ethical standards of any legal industry'.

Over the last 4 decades, neoliberalism and financial capitalism have been undermining democracy in the United States and Europe. They have succeeded in two ways. First, they have created a super-wealthy elite who distort the democratic process by funding political parties and by financing intense political lobbying. The US financial industry now employs five lobbyists for every member of Congress.[43] A so-called revolving door between Washington and Wall Street has also been established which allows senior figures to alternate between key positions in government and finance. This relationship enables financial firms with long rosters of former government officials to exercise disproportionate influence over US government policy.[44] This influence also extends to other rich democracies, to a greater or lesser extent. Second, the Financial Crisis, and governments' responses to it, have generated an intensity of public anger and distrust, directed primarily at politics and politicians, which has torn the social fabric upon which democracy depends. This anger and distrust is manifesting itself in a rise in nationalism and xenophobia, a rejection of globalization, and a willingness to choose strong leaders, even when, or especially when, those leaders promise to trample upon long-established democratic ideals. A widespread sense of powerlessness and a desire on the part of many to take back some form of control over their present and future circumstances is being seized upon by populist politicians in the United States and Europe. It has resulted in the rise of far-right parties in Europe and in growing anti-EU sentiment, including the vote to leave the European Union in the 2016 Brexit Referendum in the United Kingdom. During the referendum, the 'Leave' campaign successfully characterized the EU as a danger to British democracy and immigrants as a threat to Britain's future. In the United States, public anger and disillusionment with politics resulted in the election of Donald Trump as President. Trump's grandiosity, xenophobia, lack of empathy, and willingness to scapegoat and degrade others has prompted a number of prominent clinicians to ignore the 'Goldwater rule' (which declares it unethical for psychiatrists to comment on an individual's mental state without examining them personally and having the patient's consent to make such comments), and publicly describe Trump as having 'textbook narcissistic personality disorder'.[45] During his tenure as President, Trump has provided further evidence in support of this argument. In fact, as his term in office has proceeded, mental health professionals are arguing less about whether Trump may have a dangerous personality disorder, and more about what the psychological and psychiatric professions could practically and ethically do if that were the case.[46]

Extreme wealth and extreme poverty both empower those with dangerous personality disorders. Extreme poverty leaves the world's poorest without the protection of the law and vulnerable to exploitation by those without conscience. Extreme wealth empowers those whose driving passion is the narcissistic accrual of personal riches and power regardless of the consequences for society. Disparities of wealth and poverty empower extremists at both ends of the spectrum. The result is war, exploitation, crime, civil unrest, and financial crisis. Extreme inequality generates a centrifugal effect in which society spins faster and faster out of control.

Economist David Harvey has written that a new global economic order is urgently required, based on a worthier system of governance and a nobler concept of freedom than those that neoliberalism can offer.[47] Those currently in charge of financial capitalism, however, are incapable of developing the new economic model that is needed to address the daunting challenges of global inequality that humanity now faces. Rather than tackle these challenges, the elites in the rich world are intent on perpetuating a form of capitalism which has been expressly designed to enrich themselves regardless of the consequences for present and future generations. The stakes could not be higher. John Kay warns that, '[w]hen the next crisis hits, and it will, [the] frustrated public is likely to turn, not just on politicians...or on bankers, but on the market system. What is at stake now may not just be the future of finance, but the future of capitalism.' And, he might have added, the future of democracy too. The development of a fair and ethical global economic, political, and social system, however, will clearly not emerge as long as narcissists and psychopaths continue to write the rules.

6. Hope?

...the problem before us is how to get rid of the greatest hindrance to civilization – namely, the constitutional inclination of human beings to be aggressive towards one another.
Sigmund Freud

This book has made three related arguments.

First, people with dangerous personality disorders, namely psychopaths and those with narcissistic personality disorder and paranoid personality disorder, pose a grave threat to society. This threat is greatest when people with these disorders act together and when the circumstances are such that they can influence a substantial proportion of the psychologically normal population to support them. This is particularly the case in times of war and in times of profound economic crisis. This toxic triangle of destructive leaders, susceptible followers, and conducive environments provides an insight into the dynamics of how people with these disorders come to power. Stalin, Mao, Hitler, and Pol Pot provide concrete examples of this dynamic in practice and illustrate the profoundly destructive consequences that people with these disorders can bring about. It is argued that because of the devastating effects these leaders and their regimes have had, the history of the twentieth century cannot be properly understood without acknowledging the central role that people with dangerous personality disorders played in that century's events.

This book's second argument is that democracy can be understood as a system of defenses against people with these disorders. This system of defenses comprises the rule of law, electoral democracy, the principle of liberal individualism that underpins the separation of church and state, social democracy, and legal protection for human rights. Acting together, this system of defenses not only serves as a deterrent against dangerous individuals, it also creates an ethical environment within which the majority population is less likely to support the policies that such individuals typically espouse.

This book's third argument is an argument against inequality on the basis that extremes of both poverty and wealth empower those with dangerous personality disorders. In the case of extreme poverty, the absence both of the rule of law and of checks on those in positions of authority results in an environment in which the most ruthless gravitate toward the center of power while those with conscience and morals are flung to the margins. Extremes of wealth also undermine democracy. The concentration of wealth in the hands of a minority allows the wealthy greater access to power – through lobbying, the financing of elections, and through blatant corruption. Extreme disparities in wealth and poverty undermine the social fabric of society and give rise to a marginalized and disaffected underclass, which can turn its anger on the ruling elites. While high levels of inequality are the norm in monarchies, sultanates, kleptocracies, and dictatorships, the reduction of inequalities is one of the explicit goals of democratic government.

This book will close by introducing a fourth argument. At the beginning of the twenty-first century, a strengthening of democracy is urgently required, through a commitment to the values that underpin democracy, if human progress is to continue, immense human suffering is to be avoided, and perhaps even if humanity is to survive, in the decades to come.

A Snapshot of the Present Time

In one disturbing respect the situation today resembles that at the beginning of the twentieth century. At that time, the injustices of capitalism gave rise to widespread public anger in countries across the world and prompted the rise of the global communist movement. It took the unfathomable suffering of two world wars for a more just and inclusive accommodation between capitalism and society to be reached. This accommodation included social democracy and the assumption by the state of responsibility for limiting inequalities and protecting individual human rights. Today this accommodation between capitalism and society is unravelling. The predominance of neoliberalism as the guiding economic and political ideology has resulted in a 40-year period during which the role of the state – particularly in limiting inequalities – has been eroded. Over that same period, the fundamental nature of capitalism has radically altered. It has changed from a predominantly industrial capitalist system based on the development of new technologies and industries, to a system of financial capitalism based on making money from money. While the benefits of the former were relatively widely spread, at least within the countries of the developed world, those of the latter are being captured by an increasingly wealthy minority. The Financial Crisis of 2008, and the way in which public monies were used to bail out financial institutions while those at the head of those institutions walked away with enormous financial rewards, has undermined public confidence in both capitalism and politics. This has produced an environment in many countries within which leaders stoking racism, nationalism, and xenophobia are finding a ready audience. Their successes are eroding the foundations of democracy even further.

One way in which the current global situation differs from that a century ago, however, lies in the fact that the gap between rich developed and poor underdeveloped nations today is narrowing. In fact, it is doing so at the fastest rate since the gap first opened up at the beginning of the Industrial Revolution over 2 centuries ago. A dramatic reduction in global poverty and a rise in the health, wellbeing, and living standards of many across the developing world, particularly in China and India, is one of the hallmarks of the present time. This economic convergence marks an immense reduction in human suffering, and could lead to a reduction in war and violence and an increase in the capacity of citizens around the world to hold their governments to account. From a psychological perspective, economic convergence is akin to the tide going out on those with dangerous personality disorders, as development reduces their opportunities to gain influence and exploit others for personal gain.

However, a major challenge to continued convergence, and to the level of development of rich nations too, has arisen. It is a challenge not envisaged a century ago – the challenge of global warming. The technologies that have powered economic growth over the last 2 centuries have been producing gases, principally carbon dioxide, which are being trapped in the earth's atmosphere and are causing our planet to heat up. Global warming is already evident in the increased frequency of severe weather events, in rising sea levels, in the melting of the polar ice caps, and in the reduction of arable land in many parts of the world. Unless we act to reduce carbon emissions now, global warming is predicted to have catastrophic consequences for humanity in the century ahead.

At the beginning of the twenty-first century, we therefore find ourselves in a position where one facet of capitalism – financial capitalism – is fueling increasing levels of inequality, while the other facet – industrial capitalism – is destroying the global habitat upon which we depend. This is a crisis of capitalism orders of magnitude greater than that which the world experienced a century ago.

Other daunting challenges exist too. The sectarian war that has been raging across the Middle East between Sunni and Shia Muslims, of which ISIS is the latest deadly manifestation, continues to intensify. Authoritarianism is on the rise. Between 2000 and 2015, democracy broke down in 27 countries, among them Kenya, Russia, Thailand, and Turkey.[1] The Organisation for Economic Cooperation and Development highlights other

challenges we face.[2] The world's population is set to continue
to grow and is expected to reach 10,000,000,000 by 2050. Africa
will account for more than half of this growth, so that by 2100
Africans will account for more than one in three of the world's
population. The Middle East too will experience rapid population
growth. The countries in both these regions, of course, are already
struggling to provide education and employment for their young
people. Continued lack of employment opportunities, alongside
increased risks of internal conflict, may lead to greater instability
and force many to seek better lives and safety elsewhere.
Successfully addressing the challenge of climate change will
require the development and deployment of new low carbon
technologies and the widespread adoption of these technologies,
particularly in the developing world. This will in turn require an
unprecedented increase in international cooperation in support
of technology and knowledge transfer. It will also require the
governments of developing countries to make unprecedented
levels of investment in the scientific and technological skills
of their own populations. Finally, new technologies will bring
major risks as well as solutions in the century ahead. Martin
Rees, the UK Astronomer Royal, has issued a stark warning on
the potential dangers of new technology. Until now, Rees warns,
superpowers alone have had the capacity to destroy civilization.
'New science will soon empower small groups, even individuals',
Rees writes, 'with similar leverage over society.'[3]

Capitalism in profound crisis, global warming, population
growth allied to resource scarcity, widespread forced migration,
and increasing technological capability for both good and ill
– these are the very real challenges we face at this moment in
human history. Given such daunting prospects, it is easy to
envisage the twenty-first century as one in which, once again,
fear mongers and demagogues will prevail. But alongside these
dangers, our current moment in history is also one of promise
and hope.

The Promise of the Twenty-First Century

Historians can offer us a sense of perspective that politics often lacks because the time scale of history helps to put our present moment into a broader perspective. Ian Mortimer's magnificent book *Centuries of Change* describes the many ways in which European societies have changed over the past 1,000 years.[4] In his whistle stop tour, he shows just how much we have progressed over that time. The twelfth century saw the beginnings of codified law in Europe, under church authority, with the founding of the first school of law in Bologna. In the thirteenth century, education and literacy saw major increases and Europe's first universities were established. The century also saw the first steps toward limiting the power of kings, with the signing of the Magna Carta in England. After the tragedy of the Black Death in the fourteenth century, the fifteenth century was a century of remarkable discovery. With the voyages of Bartholomew Dias, Christopher Columbus, Vasco da Gama, and Pedro Cabral, Europeans discovered North and South America, charted the southern half of Africa, and established a seaborne route to India. In the sixteenth century, the increasing effectiveness of states in upholding the rule of law had a marked effect in reducing interpersonal violence. This brought about a transformation in people's lives, as violence became much less a feature of everyday life than it had been for previous generations. Journeys of discovery continued, most notably when Ferdinand Magellan first circumnavigated the world. European voyages of discovery, however, also resulted in misery for many of the peoples in the newly discovered lands. By 1600, for example, the transatlantic slave trade had begun. The seventeenth century saw the beginning of the Scientific Revolution and a step change in humanity's ability to control famine and disease. During the course of this century, Galileo's discoveries revolutionized our understanding of our place in the natural world and Isaac Newton demonstrated that the universe operated on mathematical laws that could be understood by man. The Industrial Revolution began in the eighteenth century, which was also, of course, a century of political revolutions. The US and French revolutions introduced the idea of the political equality of all and began to put that idea into practice. The nineteenth century was a century of invention as railways, steam ships, telegrams, the telephone, and radio communication connected the world as never before. The discovery that cholera was transmitted through infected water led to major improvements in public health. The century also witnessed the end of the trans-Atlantic slave trade, the abolition of slavery, and major advances in democracy as the franchise was extended first to men and then, gradually, to women. The nineteenth century was also the century of Darwin, Marx, and Freud – thinkers whose ideas continue to shape the world today. Finally, the twentieth century was another century of breathtaking change. Despite the devastation caused by the century's despots, it saw major improvements in literacy and women's rights and further reductions in poverty and destitution. It was a century of decolonization and the further spread of democracy. In 1900, half a dozen empires ruled most of the world. By 2000, democratic and near-democratic countries accounted for nearly half the world's population.

In this brief overview of history, the strides we have made in terms of health, knowledge, technology, and material wellbeing stand out clearly. But what also stands out is just how far we have come in our acceptance of the fundamental equality of every human being. For most of the last 1,000 years, it was widely accepted that kings ruled by divine right, that women were mentally inferior to men, and that Europeans had a right to exploit the 'inferior' peoples of the world. For centuries, working slaves to death was an acceptable way to run an economy. As the context has changed, however, so too have our values and behaviors. This is nowhere more apparent than in the progress we have made in overturning the oppressive beliefs and practices toward one another that persisted for millennia. Progress is mixed, of course, and the struggle for equality continues. But today, as never before in human history, cultural values regarding race, gender, and sexual orientation that constrain human development and prevent the majority of humanity from becoming fully human are increasingly being overturned.

Race

...when the history books are written [in future generations], the historians will [have to pause and] say: 'There lived a great people – a black people who injected new meaning and dignity into the veins of civilization.'

Martin Luther King

Today Martin Luther King and Nelson Mandela are honored as heroes and their civil rights and anti-apartheid campaigns are celebrated as having ended appalling injustices. But for most of history, the racist beliefs against which they fought were almost universally accepted in white societies. The Americas were built on the premise of white racial superiority. For 3 centuries after Columbus, an average of three Africans were hunted down and shipped into slavery for every European who set out freely for the Americas.[5] Racist beliefs persisted in white societies long after the slave trade was abolished. In 1906 the Bronx Zoo in New York exhibited a pygmy man from the Congo, Ota Benga, in a cage alongside an orang-utan to demonstrate that black Africans were closer to apes than they were to whites.[6] The *Encyclopaedia Britannica* in its 1911 edition stated as fact that, 'Mentally the negro is inferior to the white.'[7] The legacy of racism lasted well into the twentieth century and formed the basis for colonial occupation of much of the world by European powers. Even after the end of colonialism, racism remained entrenched in law in a number of countries – most notably the United States and South Africa.

The exclusion of blacks from full participation in society in the southern United States continued right up until the civil rights campaign of the 1960s, and persists even today. In South Africa, ruled by a white government elected by a whites-only electorate, the laws of apartheid similarly restricted and regulated every facet of life for non-whites. It is sobering to remind ourselves that the attitudes and practices in these last outposts of white supremacy were the accepted norm everywhere at the beginning of the last century.

Sexual Orientation

For me this struggle is a seamless robe. Opposing apartheid was a matter of justice. Opposing discrimination against women is a matter of justice. Opposing discrimination on the basis of sexual orientation is a matter of justice.
Desmond Tutu

A second major shift in values can be seen in the marked reduction in discrimination against sexual minorities. In the 1950s, laws banned gay people from federal employment in the United States. Due to the classification of homosexuality by the psychiatric profession as a mental disorder, thousands of gay men were involuntarily committed to mental institutions, where many were forced to undergo electroshock treatment in an attempt to cure them of their 'disease'. The Stonewall riot of 1969, which took place in response to a police raid at the Stonewall Inn in New York City, is widely seen as the beginning of the modern gay rights movement. In the few short decades since Stonewall, the cultures in many countries have changed to become markedly more tolerant of homosexuality. In 1993, post-apartheid South Africa became the first country ever to include in its constitution the prohibition of discrimination on the grounds of sexual orientation. In 2001, the Netherlands became the first country in the world to legalize same-sex marriages. Despite remarkable progress, however, in other parts of the world the level of hostility toward lesbians and gay men is such that coming out openly as homosexual still carries the threat of imprisonment or execution. In 76 countries gay people face imprisonment for forming same-sex relationships.[8] Seven countries have laws that threaten gay people with execution – Iran, Mauritania, Saudi Arabia, Yemen, Sudan, Somalia, and Nigeria.[9]

Gender

I do not wish them to have power over men, but over themselves.
Mary Wollstonecraft

For centuries women have been struggling to achieve a wide range of fundamental rights – the right to education; the right to choose a husband rather than having him chosen by others; the right to initiate divorce rather than this being the exclusive preserve of men; the right to bodily integrity, including the right to refuse sex within marriage; the right to choose whether and when to bear children; the right to work and receive equal pay to men; the right to vote; and the right to be acknowledged as full citizens in law. As is the case with race and sexual orientation, enormous progress has been made. Of all the world's injustices, however, continued refusal to recognize women as equal to men carries the highest costs in terms of suffering and loss of life. In poor societies, males who serve as the main breadwinners are generally regarded as being of greater value than females. As a result, scarce resources such as food and healthcare are reserved mainly for men and boys. Nobel Prize-winning economist Amartya Sen has estimated that this anti-female bias has resulted in the premature deaths of over 100 million girls and women worldwide.[10] Sexist cultures also underpin a vast illicit sex trade. The number of women and girls being trafficked into sexual slavery every year is now much higher than the number of slaves shipped across the Atlantic annually during the height of the slave trade in the eighteenth century.[11] Sexist cultures also contribute to the persistence of poverty and to high levels of violence against women. Two-thirds of the world's poorest people today – those living on less than one dollar a day – are women.

We stand, therefore, at a remarkable moment in history. Never before has humanity as a whole enjoyed the levels of health and material wellbeing that we do today. Never before have so many individuals had the freedom to develop their full potential regardless of their race, gender, sexual orientation, or the myriad other ways in which we vary. But for very, very many people the fruits of progress are still beyond reach, as their lives continue to be blighted by poverty, violence, discrimination, and injustice. And never before has humanity faced the level of existential threat that we currently face.

Hope?

It is clear that if we are to successfully negotiate our way through the dangers of the present moment, resolve the daunting challenges we face, and realize the opportunities for progress that continued human development for all offers us, a very different world order is needed. Astonishingly, given the current levels of war, violence, and inequality that scar our world, the blueprint for this new world order not only exists, but has been agreed by almost every country on earth. In 2015 the United Nations unanimously adopted 17 Sustainable Development Goals and a vision for the type of world that these goals aim to achieve.[12]

The vision the UN Sustainable Development Goals sets out is one of a world free of poverty, hunger, disease, and want, a world free from fear and violence. It is a world with universal access to education, to health care, and social protection, where every person's physical, mental, and social well-being is assured. It is a world of universal respect for human rights and human dignity, the rule of law, justice, equality, and non-discrimination; of respect for race, ethnicity, and cultural diversity; a world of equal opportunity permitting the full realization of human potential and contributing to shared prosperity. It is a world which invests in its children, in which every child grows up free from violence and exploitation; a world in which every woman and girl enjoys full gender equality and all barriers to their empowerment have been removed. It is a just, equitable, tolerant, open, and socially inclusive world in which the needs of the most vulnerable are met. It is a world in which every country enjoys sustained, inclusive, and sustainable economic growth and decent work for all; a world in which consumption and production patterns are sustainable; it is a world in which humanity lives in harmony with nature and in which other living species are protected.

That the world's nations have reached agreement on what constitutes a better world is a remarkable achievement. At a time when war and suffering are ever present in our headlines, it is a much-needed beacon of hope. But those very pictures of war and suffering also beg the question: are we, humanity, psychologically capable of building such a fair and more peaceful world? While all governments of the world have, in principle, signed up to this vision, there is a minority in every society on earth, many of whom hold positions of power, for whom a world of greater equality, of peace, of human rights, and dignity for all, is an anathema. Their psychology compels them to create an environment in which their superiority, their paranoia, their dehumanization and exploitation of others, is the norm. Which brings us to this book's fourth argument: at the beginning of the twenty-first century, a strengthening of democracy is urgently required, through a commitment to the values that underpin democracy, if human progress is to continue, immense human suffering is to be avoided, and perhaps even if humanity is to survive in the decades to come.

The presence of people with dangerous personality disorders in our midst continues to fundamentally alter the swing of the pendulum in the conduct of human affairs from compromise to conflict, from inclusion to vilification, and from humanity toward savagery. It is clear, however, that there is no simple solution to the problem. Our religions, our economics, our politics, and our ideas of leadership are currently too intertwined with values of domination, dogma, and inequality to admit any ready solutions. Whatever further means we devise to reduce the influence of those with these disorders must dampen the swing of the pendulum, rather than exacerbate it. The strongest protection is the most obvious – to ensure that individuals with dangerous personality disorders do not achieve positions of power or influence at any level of society – within communities, within organizations, or within nations. This is easier said than done. Given the illusive nature of these disorders, and the fact that single individuals are never the sole cause of the problem, a witch hunt targeting those suspected of having dangerous personality disorders is neither feasible nor desirable.

Instead, a strengthening of democracy, and the values that underpin it, is the most effective action we can take to further reduce the influence of people with dangerous personality disorders. Such action can be effective because it addresses all three sides of the toxic triangle of toxic leaders, susceptible followers, and conducive environments. As we have seen, democracy places limits on those in power. It reduces the scope for recourse to violence on the part of ruling elites. It forbids the abuse of state power against individuals and against sub-sections of society. It subjects those in power to the rule of law. In this way it provides a powerful constraint on the destructive actions of individuals and groups with these disorders. Democracy also produces public goods that include peace, justice, freedom, equality, and community. These public goods play a decisive role in influencing the behavior of the psychologically normal majority by containing the worst aspects of human nature. Strengthening democracy, therefore, addresses the other two sides of the toxic triangle by preventing environments that are conducive to people with dangerous personality disorders, and by reducing the ranks of susceptible followers from within the psychologically normal population.

Human rights activist and statesman Vaclav Havel wrote that within every person there is an innate drive for dignity, for moral integrity, for free expression of being, but at the same time every person is capable to a greater or lesser degree of living with a profane trivialization of their humanity.[13] When prevailing cultures trivialize people's humanity, Havel continued, we unconsciously create defenses that allow us to live with ourselves and the compromises we have settled for. The result is a world of scapegoating, trauma, mental illness, depression, and unfulfilled human potential. Such is the world that people with dangerous personality disorders create by constraining human development within an environment of brutality, oppression, and paranoia. In sharp contrast, democracy, as R.H. Tawney wrote, aims for 'the utmost possible development of every human being and the deliberate organization of society for the attainment of that objective.'[14]

This book is a defense of democracy, but not simply as an end in itself, not as a means of enrichment for a few, not even as a means to material progress, although it can be that too. This book is a defense of democracy because it is the political and the moral system which best allows every human being to grow to fulfill their potential. And it is from within such a democratic society – comprising flourishing individuals within a flourishing society – that progress can most readily arise. The future of humanity and the future of democracy are deeply intertwined. It is our best hope for a more humane and meaningful world. Only through democracy can we ensure that hope and history rhyme.

6. Hope?

There is no iron law of progress in human history, of course. The outcome of the struggle between the majority of humanity and the pathologically disordered minority who distort our societies is still uncertain. It is possible that death camps such as those of Nazism and Communism, the genocides of the Holocaust and Rwanda, the murderous civil wars of Africa and the Middle East, and the inhuman reigns of terror of the world's tyrants could all be consigned to history for ever. The outcome could be one in which religions remain a meaningful part of people's lives without degenerating into sectarianism. People could differ in their cultural values without those differences becoming a source of discrimination and exclusion. Capitalism could be made to work in the interests of economic growth and global cohesion by taming financial capitalism and tapping the ingenuity of all of the world's people for the development of the new technologies needed to address the defining challenges of global warming and global inequality. Global poverty could be eliminated through a combination of economic growth in developing countries, based on the transfer of technology to these countries, and a more equitable redistribution of existing global wealth.

However, this outcome can only be achieved if people with dangerous personality disorders are removed from positions of influence and power and safeguards are put in place to ensure that such pathological individuals cannot again assume authority over us. Given the scale of suffering they cause, and the existential challenges we now face, devising the means to reduce this dangerous minority's malignant influence is the overriding moral imperative in the century ahead.

Author Biography

Ian Hughes is a writer, researcher, and policy advisor in science, technology, and innovation. He has a PhD in Physics and a Postgraduate Diploma in Psychoanalytic Psychotherapy. His writing on personality disorders has appeared on the Psychology Today and Open Democracy websites. His blog disorderedworld. com focuses on dangerous personality disorders and their consequences and has been shortlisted several times in the top political blogs in Ireland. He is based in Dublin, Ireland.

Note to Reader

Thank you for reading *Disordered Minds*. My aim in writing this book is to increase awareness of how a small minority of people with dangerous personality disorders are shaping our world in a way that normalizes violence and greed. It is my sincere hope that a greater understanding of these disorders can help shape a different world, a world based on respect for the dignity of every person. If you have views on what you have read, please visit my website www.disorderedworld.com and join the conversation. I would also appreciate if you could add your review of *Disordered Minds* at your favorite online site. Your actions in defense of democracy are vital if we are to change our world for the better.

Ian Hughes

References

Chapter 1

1. Sigmund Freud, 'Civilisation and Its Discontents', in *The Standard Edition of the Complete Psychological Works of Sigmund Freud, Volume XXI (1927–1931)*, Vintage, 2001: 110
2. In the same place: 112
3. Hannah Arendt, *Eichmann in Jerusalem: A report on the banality of evil*, Penguin Classics, 2006
4. Sigmund Freud, 'Civilisation and Its Discontents', in *The Standard Edition of the Complete Psychological Works of Sigmund Freud, Volume XXI (1927–1931)*, Vintage, 2001: 122
5. Philip G. Zimbardo, 'The Banality of Evil, the Banality of Heroism', in *What is Your Dangerous Idea?*, John Brockman (ed.), Pocket Books, 2007: 282
6. A.N. Schore, *Affect Regulation and the Origin of the Self: The Neurobiology of Emotional Development*, Psychology Press, 1999
7. Sue Gerhardt, *Why Love Matters: How affection shapes a baby's brain*, Routledge, 2015
8. Hervey Cleckley, *The Mask of Sanity: An attempt to reinterpret the so-called psychopathic personality*, C.V. Mosby, 1941
9. Robert Linder, *Rebel Without a Cause*, Grove Press Inc., 1944
10. Theodore Millon, *Disorders of Personality*, Wiley, 1981
11. Robert D. Hare, *Without Conscience: The disturbing world of the psychopaths among us*, The Guilford Press, 1993
12. Mary McMurran and Richard Howard (eds), *Personality, Personality Disorder and Violence*, Wiley-Blackwell, 2009: 5
13. Martha Stout, *The Sociopath Next Door*, Broadway, 2006
14. Robert D. Hare, *Without Conscience: The disturbing world of the psychopaths among us*, The Guilford Press, 1993: 43
15. In the same place: 87
16. In the same place: 92

17. Jennifer L. Skeem, Devon L. L. Polaschek, Christopher J. Patrick and Scott O. Lilienfeld, 'Psychopathic Personality: Bridging the Gap Between Scientific Research and Public Policy', *Psychological Science in the Public Interest*, December 2011, vol. 12. no. 3.

18. J.M. Post, 'Current concepts of the narcissistic personality: Implications for political psychology', *Political Psychology*, Vol, 14, No. 1, 1993: 110

19. Wilfred R. Bion, *Transformations*, Heinemann, 1965

20. Betty Glad, 'Why Tyrants Go Too Far: Narcissism and Absolute Power', *Political Psychology*, Vol. 23, No.1, March 2002: 1–37

21. Fritz Redlich, *Hitler: Diagnosis of a Destructive Prophet*, Oxford University Press, 1998

22. Michael M. Sheng, 'Mao Zedong's narcissistic personality disorder and China's road to disaster', in *Profiling Political Leaders: Cross-cultural studies of personality and behavior*, O. Feldman and L.O. Valenty, Praeger, 2001: 116

23. Karl Popper, *Lesson of This Century: With two talks on Freedom and The Democratic State*, Interviewed by Giancarlo Bosetti, Routledge, 2007: 43

24. Andrew M. Lobaczewski, *Political Ponerology: A science on the nature of evil for political purposes*, Red Pill Press, 2009

25. In the same place: 127

26. See for example Sankowsky D, (1995), 'The charismatic leader as narcissist: Understanding the abuse of power, Organisational Dynamics', 23(4): 57–71; Maccoby M., (2000), 'Narcissistic leaders', *Harvard Business Review*, 78(1): 68–78

27. Eric Hoffer, *The True Believer: Thoughts on the Nature of Mass Movements*, Harper Perennial, Reissue Edition, 2009: 80

28. In the same place: 100

29. In the same place: 11

30. Quoted in Jerrold M. Post, *Narcissism and Politics: Dreams of glory*, Cambridge University Press, 2015: xi

31. Such authors include Paul Babiak and Robert D. Hare, authors of *Snakes in Suits: When psychopaths go to work*, HarperBusiness, 2007; Martha Stout, *The Sociopath Next Door*, Broadway, 2005; Alan Goldman, author of *Transforming Toxic Leaders*, Kogan Page, 2009; Manfred F.R. Kets de Vries, author of *Organisations on the Couch: Clinical perspectives on organisational behavior and change*, Jossey-Bass, 1991; Jerrold M Post, author of *Narcissism and Politics: Dreams of glory*, Cambridge University Press, 2015; and Vamik D. Volkan, author of *The Need to Have Enemies & Allies: From Clinical Practice to International Relationships*, Jason Aronson Inc. Publishers, 1988.

32. Daniel Jonah Goldhagen, *Hitler's Willing Executioners: Ordinary Germans and the Holocaust*, Alfred A. Knopf, 1996: 166

33. James Waller, *Becoming Evil: How ordinary people commit genocide and mass killing*, Oxford University Press, 2002: 14

34. N. Kteily, E. Bruneau, A. Waytz and S. Cotterill, 'The ascent of man: Theoretical and empirical evidence for blatant dehumanisation', *J. Pers. Soc. Psychol.*, 109 (5), 2015: 901–931

35. Kent A. Kiehl and Joshua W. Buckholtz, 'Inside the Mind of a Psychopath', *Scientific American Mind*, September / October 2010: 28

36. Mary McMurran and Richard Howard (eds), *Personality, Personality Disorder and Violence*, Wiley-Blackwell, 2009: 90

37. B.F. Grant, D.S. Hasin, and F.S. Stinson, 'Prevalence, Correlates, and Disability of Personality Disorders in the United States: Results from the National Epidemiologic Survey On Alcohol and Related Conditions', *Year Book of Psychiatry & Applied Mental Health*, January 2006: 133–134

38. Fernando Savater, *Amador: in which a father addresses his son on questions of ethics – That is, the options and values of freedom*, Henry Holt and Company Inc., 1996

Chapter 2

1. Stephane Courtois, Nicolas Werth, Jean-Louis Panne, Andrzej Paczkowski, Karel Bartosek and Jean-Louis Margolin, *The Black Book of Communism: Crimes, Terror, Repression*, Harvard University Press, 1999

2. Simon Sebag Montefiore, *Stalin: The Court of the Red Tsar*, Phoenix, 2004

3. In the same place: 235

4. Quoted in Sheila Fitzpatrick, *The Russian Revolution*, Oxford University Press, Second Edition, 1994: 98

5. Simon Sebag Montefiore, *Stalin: The Court of the Red Tsar*, Phoenix, 2004: 5

6. Robert Service, *Trotsky: A Biography*, Macmillan, 2009

7. Simon Sebag Montefiore, *Stalin: The Court of the Red Tsar*, Phoenix, 2003: 47

8. Quoted in Simon Sebag Montefiore, *Stalin: The Court of the Red Tsar*, Phoenix, 2004: 27

9. Quoted in Sheila Fitzpatrick, *The Russian Revolution*, Oxford University Press, Second Edition, 1994: 130

10. Orlando Figes, *The Whisperers: Private Life in Stalin's Russia*, Penguin Books, 2007: 80

11. In the same place: 95

12. Vasily Grossman, *Forever Flowing*, Northwestern University Press, 2000: 142

13. Orlando Figes, *The Whisperers: Private Life in Stalin's Russia*, Penguin Books, 2007: 98

14. In the same place: 99

15. Robert S. Robins and Jerrold M. Post, *Political Paranoia: The Psychopolitics of Hatred*, Yale University Press, 1997: 24

16. Simon Sebag Montefiore, *Stalin: The Court of the Red Tsar*, Phoenix, 2004: 234

17. Orlando Figes, *The Whisperers: Private Life in Stalin's Russia*, Penguin Books, 2007: 241

18. Anne Applebaum, *Gulag: A History*, Penguin Books, 2003:

105

19. Simon Sebag Montefiore, *Stalin: The Court of the Red Tsar*, Phoenix, 2003: 236

20. Quoted in Simon Sebag Montefiore, *Stalin: The Court of the Red Tsar*, Phoenix, 2004: 234

21. A.J.P. Taylor, *The Warlords*, Penguin Books, 1977: 103

22. In the same place: 124

23. Anne Applebaum, *Gulag: A History*, Penguin Books, 2003: 394

24. In the same place: 376

25. Khruschev, N.S., *Khruschev Remembers*, (S. Talbott, Trans., ed.) Boston: Little, Brown, 1970, quoted in Betty Glad, 'Why Tyrants Go Too Far: Malignant narcissists and absolute power', *Political Psychology*, Vol 23, No.1, March 2002

26. Quoted in Anne Applebaum, *Gulag: A History*, Penguin Books, 2003: 429

27. Quoted in Richard McGregor, *The Party: The secret world of China's Communist Rulers*, Allen Lane, 2010: 246

28. Quoted in Jung Chang and Jon Halliday, *Mao: The unknown story*, Vintage, 2006: 42

29. In the same place: 13

30. Quoted in Jung Chang and Jon Halliday, *Mao: The unknown story*, Vintage, 2006: 14

31. In the same place: 14

32. In the same place: 338

33. In the same place: 453

34. In the same place: 458

35. Karl Popper, *Lesson of This Century: With two talks on Freedom and The Democratic State*, Interviewed by Giancarlo Bosetti, Routledge, 2007: 83

36. Herbert Bix, *Hirohito and the Making of Modern Japan*, Harper Collins, 2001: 55

37. Ian Buruma, *The Wages of Guilt: Memories of War in Germany and Japan*, Atlantic Books, 2009: 121

38. Laurence Rees, *Horror in the East*, BBC Books, 2011: 33
39. In the same place: 38
40. Herbert P. Bix, *Hirohito and the Making of Modern Japan*, Harper Collins, 2001: 367
41. James Dawes, *Evil Men*, Harvard University Press, 2013: 65
42. In the same place: 26
43. In the same place: 40
44. Laurence Rees, *Horror in the East*, BBC Books, 2011: 47
45. Frank Dikotter, *The Tragedy of Liberation: A history of the Chinese Revolution 1945–57*, Bloomsbury, 2013: 25
46. John Byron and Robert Pack, *The Claws of the Dragon: Kang Sheng, the evil genius behind Mao and his legacy of terror in People's China*, Simon and Schuster, 1992
47. Frank Dikotter, *The Tragedy of Liberation: A history of the Chinese Revolution 1945–57*, Bloomsbury, 2013: xiii
48. Frank Dikotter, *Mao's Great Famine: The history of China's most devastating catastrophe, 1958–1962,* Bloomsbury Publishing Plc, 2010: 50
49. Frank Dikotter, *The Tragedy of Liberation: A history of the Chinese Revolution 1945–57*, Bloomsbury, 2013: 197
50. Frank Dikotter, *Mao's Great Famine*, Bloomsbury, 2011: 32
51. In the same place: 103
52. In the same place: 302
53. In the same place: 248
54. Frank Dikotter, Mao's Great Famine: *The history of China's most devastating catastrophe, 1958–1962*, Bloomsbury, 2010
55. In the same place: 252
56. In the same place: 41
57. Quoted in Frank Dikotter, *The Tragedy of Liberation: A history of the Chinese Revolution 1945–57*, Bloomsbury, 2013: 94

Chapter 3

1. Ian Kershaw, *Hitler: 1889–1936: Hubris*, Norton, 1998
2. Quoted in Betty Glad, 'Why Tyrants Go Too Far: Malignant

narcissists and absolute power', *Political Psychology*, Vol. 23, No.1, March 2002: 1–37

3. Roger Osborne, *Of the People, By the People, A new history of democracy*, Bodley Head, 2011: 192
4. In the same place: 198
5. Timothy Snyder, *Blood Lands, Europe between Hitler and Stalin*, Bodley Head, 2010: 163
6. In the same place: 254
7. In the same place: 187
8. Anthony Read, *The Devil's Disciples: The lives and times of Hitler's inner circle*, Pimlico, 2003: 757
9. Philip Short, *Pol Pot, The history of a nightmare*, John Murray Publishers, 2004: 338
10. In the same place: 339
11. David P. Chandler, Ben Kiernan and Chanthou Boua, *Pol Pot Plans the Future: Confidential Leadership Documents from Democratic Kampuchea, 1976–1977*, Yale Southeast Asia Studies Monograph Series, 1988
12. In the same place
13. Philip Short, *Pol Pot, The history of a nightmare*, John Murray Publishers, 2004: 317
14. In the same place: 309
15. Rithy Panh, *The Elimination*, The Clerkenwell Press, 2013: 34
16. In the same place: 57
17. Philip Short, Pol Pot, *The history of a nightmare*, John Murray Publishers, 2004: 364
18. Quoted in Rithy Panh, *The Elimination*, The Clerkenwell Press, 2013: 117
19. Philip Short, Pol Pot, *The history of a nightmare*, John Murray Publishers, 2004: 387
20. In the same place: 401
21. In the same place: 365
22. Mark T. Mitchell, *Michael Polanyi*, ISI Books, 2006: xi
23. Jerrold M. Post, 'Current concepts of the narcissistic

personality: Implications for political psychology', *Political Psychology*, Vol. 14, No.1, March 1993: 99–121

24. Art Padilla, Robert Hogan and Robert B. Kaiser, 'The toxic triangle: Destructive leaders, susceptible followers and conducive followers', *The Leadership Quarterly*, 18 (2007), 176–194

25. Jerrold M. Post, 'Book Review: Hitler: Diagnosis of a destructive prophet', *N Engl J Med* 1999, 340: 1691–1692

Chapter 4

1. Anne Applebaum, *Gulag: A history of the Soviet camps*, Penguin, 2004: 514

2. Economist Intelligence Unit Democracy Index 2016

3. Adam Swift, *Political Philosophy: A beginners' guide for students and politicians,* Second Edition, Polity Press, 2007: 203

4. In the same place: 217

5. Stephen Pinker, *The Better Angels of Our Nature: A history of violence and humanity*, Penguin, 2012

6. Tom Bingham, *The Rule of Law*, Penguin Books, 2010

7. In the same place: 14

8. Roger Osborne, *Of the People, By the People: A new history of democracy*, Bodley Head, 2011: 98

9. John Jay, *The Correspondence and Public Papers of John Jay*, Henry P. Johnston, ed., G.P. Putnams Sons, 1890, Vol. I, 161

10. Adam Swift, *Political Philosophy: A beginners' guide for students and politicians*, Second Edition, Polity Press, 2007: 140

11. Jeffry A. Frieden, *Global Capitalism: Its fall and rise in the twentieth century*, W.W. Norton and Company Ltd, 2006: 167

12. In the same place: 210

13. Sheri Berman, *The Primacy of Politics: Social democracy and the making of Europe's twentieth century*, Cambridge University Press, 2006

14. Quoted in Paul Gordon Lauren, *The Evolution of International Human Rights: Visions Seen*, University of Pennsylvania Press, 2003: 202

15. Anne Applebaum, *Iron Curtain: The crushing of Eastern Europe, 1944–1956*, Allen Lane, 2012

16. In the same place: 113

17. In the same place: 117

18. In the same place: 226

19. In the same place: 180

20. In the same place: 184

21. Quoted in Anne Applebaum, *Iron Curtain: The crushing of Eastern Europe, 1944–1956*, Allen Lane, 2012: 184

22. Anne Applebaum, *Iron Curtain: The crushing of Eastern Europe, 1944–1956*, Allen Lane, 2012: 296

23. In the same place: 313

24. In the same place: 496

25. M.F.R. Kets de Vries, 'The spirit of despotism: Understanding the tyrant within', *Human Relations*, February 2006, 59, 2: 203

26. In the same place: 219

Chapter 5

1. Paul Collier, *The Bottom Billion: Why the poorest countries are failing and what can be done about it*, Oxford University Press, 2007: 7

2. Gary A. Haugen and Victor Boutros, *The Locust Effect*, Oxford University Press, 2014: 18

3. In the same place: 18

4. Richard Dowden, *Africa: Altered States, Ordinary Miracles*, Portobello Books Ltd, 2008: 372

5. Jason Stearns, *Dancing in the Glory of Monsters*, Public Affairs, 2012

6. In the same place: 331

7. Amartya Sen, *The Argumentative Indian: Writings on Indian Culture, History and Identity*, Penguin Books, 2006: 302

8. Gary A. Haugen and Victor Boutros, *The Locust Effect*, Oxford University Press, 2014: 43
9. In the same place: 126
10. Nicholas D. Kristof and Sheryl Wudunn, *Half the Sky: How to change the world*, Virago, 2010
11. Radha Vinod Raja, *Fighting Corruption: How serious is India?* Institute of Peace and Conflict Studies Issue Brief Number 158, New Delhi, December 2010
12. Sarah Chayes, *Thieves of State: Why corruption threatens global security*, W.W. Norton & Company, 2015: 62
13. 'Corruption in Afghanistan: Recent Patterns and Trends', United Nations Office on Drugs and Crime (UNODC), 2012: 17
14. 'Corruption and Insecurity in Nigeria, Musa Idris', Public Administration Research, Vol. 2, No. 1, 2013: 59
15. Angus Deaton, *The Great Escape: Health, wealth and the origins of inequality*, Princeton University Press, 2013
16. William J. Baumol, *The Free-Market Innovation Machine: Analyzing the Growth Miracle of Capitalism*, Princeton University Press, 2004: 3
17. Angus Deaton, *The Great Escape: Health, wealth and the origins of inequality*, Princeton University Press, 2013: 167
18. Oswaldo de Rivero, *The Myth of Development: Non-viable economies and the crisis of civilisation*, Zed Books, 2010: 46
19. In the same place: 29
20. Thomas M. Hoenig, 'Do SIFIs Have a Future?' Speech to New York University Stern School of Business, 27 June 2011: 2
21. Dani Rodrik, *The Globalisation Paradox: Why global markets, states and democracy can't coexist*, Oxford University Press, 2011: 90
22. In the same place: 107
23. Alex Callinicos, *Bonfire of Illusions: The twin crises of the liberal world*, Polity Press, 2011: 74

186

24. http://www.pbs.org/wgbh/pages/frontline/warning/inter
    views/born.html
25. Manfred Steger, 'Globalisation and Ideology' in *The Blackwell
    Companion to Globalisation,* 2007
26. Robert J. Antonio, 'The Cultural Construction of Neoliberal
    Globalisation' in *The Blackwell Companion to Globalisation,*
    2007
27. *BusinessWeek,* 13 December 1999: 212
28. Yves Smith, *Econned: How unenlightened self-interest
    undermined democracy and corrupted capitalism,* Palgrave
    Macmillan, 2010: 171
29. Joris Luyendijk, *Swimming with Sharks: My journey into the
    world of bankers,* Guardian Books and Faber and Faber, 2015
30. Quoted in Yves Smith, *Econned: How unenlightened self-
    interest undermined democracy and corrupted capitalism,*
    Palgrave Macmillan, 2010: 150
31. Quoted in Yves Smith, *Econned: How unenlightened self-
    interest undermined democracy and corrupted capitalism,*
    Palgrave Macmillan, 2010: 134
32. Quoted in Yves Smith, *Econned: How unenlightened self-
    interest undermined democracy and corrupted capitalism,*
    Palgrave Macmillan, 2010: 135
33. Quoted in Paul Mason, Meltdown: *The end of the age of greed,*
    Verso, 2009: 4
34. Quoted in Yves Smith, *Econned: How unenlightened self-
    interest undermined democracy and corrupted capitalism,*
    Palgrave Macmillan, 2010: 129
35. Joris Luyendijk, *Swimming with Sharks: My journey into the
    world of bankers,* Guardian Books and Faber and Faber, 2015:
    232
36. Paul Babiak and Robert D. Hare, *Snakes in Suits: When
    psychopaths go to work,* Harper, 2007: 193
37. Alan Goldman, 'Personality disorders in leaders:
    Implications of the DSM IV-TR in assessing dysfunctional

organisations', *Journal of Managerial Psychology*, Vol. 21, Iss. 5, 2006: 392–414. See also Alan Goldman, *Destructive Leaders and Dysfunctional Organisations: A therapeutic approach*, Cambridge University Press, 2009

38. Quoted in Gillian Tett, *Fool's Gold: How unrestrained greed corrupted a dream, shattered global markets and unleashed a catastrophe*, Abacus, 2010: 284
39. *Inside Job*, Director Charles Ferguson, Sony Pictures, 2010
40. Sir Fred Goodwin refuses to return pension, *The Telegraph*, 26 February 2009
41. Pervasive Culture of Corruption in the Financial Services Industry Cited by Judge In Sentencing Ruling, Steven Meyerowitz, Financial Fraud Law, 01/26/2010, www.financialfraudlaw.com
42. Greg Smith, 'Why I am leaving Goldman Sachs', *New York Times*, 14 March 2012
43. *Inside Job*, Director Charles Ferguson, Sony Pictures, 2010
44. David Rothkopf, *Superclass: How the rich ruined our world*, Abacus, 2008: 149
45. Randi Kreger, 'Therapists Confirm Trump's Narcissistic Personality Disorder: Concerned therapists break silence to warn the public', 'Stop Walking on Eggshells Blog', *Psychology Today*, Posted 13 November 2015
46. *The Dangerous Case of Donald Trump: 27 Psychiatrists and Mental Health Experts Assess a President*, Bandy X. Lee (ed.), Thomas Dunne Books, 2017
47. David Harvey, *A Brief History of Neoliberalism*, Oxford University Press, 2011: 206

Chapter 6

1. Larry Diamond, 'Democracy in Decline: How Washington Can Reverse the Tide', *Foreign Affairs*, July/August 2016
2. Organisation for Economic Cooperation and Development, *OECD Science, Technology and Industry Outlook 2016*, Paris,

2016

3. Martin Rees, *Our Final Century: Will civilisation survive the twenty-first century?* Arrow, 2004

4. Ian Mortimer, *Centuries of Change: Which century saw the most change?* Bodley Head, 2014

5. David Brion Davis, *Inhuman Bondage: The rise and fall of slavery in the New World*, Oxford University Press, 2006: 80

6. Phillip V. Bradford and Harvey Blume, *Ota Benga: The Pygmy in the Zoo*, St Martins, 1992

7. Quoted in David Brion Davis, *Inhuman Bondage: The rise and fall of slavery in the New World*, Oxford University Press, 2006: 76

8. 'State-sponsored Homophobia: A world survey of laws prohibiting same-sex activity between consenting adults', Daniel Ottosson, ILGA, 2010

9. 'We Are a Buried Generation: Discrimination and Violence against Sexual Minorities in Iran', Human Rights Watch, 2010

10. Amartya Sen, *The Argumentative Indian: Writings on Indian culture, history and identity*, Penguin Books, 2006: 226

11. Nicholas D. Kristof and Sheryl Wudunn, *Half the Sky: How to change the world*, Virago Press, 2010: 12

12. *Sustainable Development Goals: Introducing the 2030 agenda for sustainable development*, United Nations Publications, 2015

13. Vaclav Havel, *The Power of the Powerless*, October 1978

14. Quoted in Roy Hattersley, *Choose Freedom: The future of democratic socialism*, Michael Joseph Ltd, 1987

Zero Books

CULTURE, SOCIETY & POLITICS

Contemporary culture has eliminated the concept and public figure of the intellectual. A cretinous anti-intellectualism presides, cheer-led by hacks in the pay of multinational corporations who reassure their bored readers that there is no need to rouse themselves from their stupor. Zer0 Books knows that another kind of discourse - intellectual without being academic, popular without being populist - is not only possible: it is already flourishing. Zer0 is convinced that in the unthinking, blandly consensual culture in which we live, critical and engaged theoretical reflection is more important than ever before.

If you have enjoyed this book, why not tell other readers by posting a review on your preferred book site.

Recent bestsellers from Zero Books are

In the Dust of This Planet
Horror of Philosophy vol. 1
Eugene Thacker
In the first of a series of three books on the Horror of
Philosophy, *In the Dust of This Planet* offers the genre of horror
as a way of thinking about the unthinkable.
Paperback: 978-1-84694-676-9 ebook: 978-1-78099-010-1

Capitalist Realism
Is there no alternative?
Mark Fisher
An analysis of the ways in which capitalism has presented itself
as the only realistic political-economic system.
Paperback: 978-1-84694-317-1 ebook: 978-1-78099-734-6

Rebel Rebel
Chris O'Leary
David Bowie: every single song. Everything you want to know,
everything you didn't know.
Paperback: 978-1-78099-244-0 ebook: 978-1-78099-713-1

Cartographies of the Absolute
Alberto Toscano, Jeff Kinkle
An aesthetics of the economy for the twenty-first century.
Paperback: 978-1-78099-275-4 ebook: 978-1-78279-973-3

Poor but Sexy
Culture Clashes in Europe East and West
Agata Pyzik
How the East stayed East and the West stayed West.
Paperback: 978-1-78099-394-2 ebook: 978-1-78099-395-9

Malign Velocities
Accelerationism and Capitalism
Benjamin Noys
Long listed for the Bread and Roses Prize 2015, *Malign Velocities*
argues against the need for speed, tracking acceleration as the
symptom of the on-going crises of capitalism.
Paperback: 978-1-78279-300-7 ebook: 978-1-78279-299-4

Meat Market
Female Flesh under Capitalism
Laurie Penny
A feminist dissection of women's bodies as the fleshy fulcrum
of capitalist cannibalism, whereby women are both consumers
and consumed.
Paperback: 978-1-84694-521-2 ebook: 978-1-84694-782-7

Romeo and Juliet in Palestine
Teaching Under Occupation
Tom Sperlinger
Life in the West Bank, the nature of pedagogy and the role of a
university under occupation.
Paperback: 978-1-78279-637-4 ebook: 978-1-78279-636-7

Sweetening the Pill
or How we Got Hooked on Hormonal Birth Control
Holly Grigg-Spall
Has contraception liberated or oppressed women? *Sweetening
the Pill* breaks the silence on the dark side of hormonal
contraception.
Paperback: 978-1-78099-607-3 ebook: 978-1-78099-608-0

Why Are We The Good Guys?
Reclaiming your Mind from the Delusions of Propaganda
David Cromwell
A provocative challenge to the standard ideology that Western
power is a benevolent force in the world.
Paperback: 978-1-78099-365-2 ebook: 978-1-78099-366-9

Readers of ebooks can buy or view any of these bestsellers by
clicking on the live link in the title. Most titles are published
in paperback and as an ebook. Paperbacks are available in
traditional bookshops. Both print and ebook formats are
available online.

Find more titles and sign up to our readers' newsletter at
http://www.johnhuntpublishing.com/culture-and-politics
Follow us on Facebook at
https://www.facebook.com/ZeroBooks
and Twitter at https://twitter.com/Zer0Books